AS REQUESTED

As Requested
The Best of Carol's Cooking Classes
Carol Ziemann

CZ Cuizine LLC
czcuizine@outlook.com

Published by Lanz Publishing Company, Ellisville, Missouri
Copyright ©2013 by Carol Ziemann
All rights reserved.

Editors Carol Ziemann, Gena Bast
Managing Editor Lyle Ziemann
Copyeditors Carol Hollenbeck, Janice Martin, Patty Tomaselli
Cover and Interior Designer Eszter Clark
Photographer Steve Adams, Steve Adams Studio, St. Louis, Missouri

Second Printing November 2013

Library of Congress Control Number 2013916600

As Requested: The Best of Carol's Cooking Classes / A Collection of Favorite Cooking Class and Treasured Family Recipes Plus Helpful Tips / Carol Ziemann
Includes index

ISBN 978-0-9899641-0-4
1. Cooking/Courses & Dishes/General   2. Cooking/Regional & Ethnic/American/General
I. Title

AS REQUESTED

THE BEST OF
CAROL'S COOKING CLASSES

Carol Ziemann

Many Thanks

First and foremost, thank you to my many cooking school students who constantly encouraged me to write this book and provided the incentive to write it. Without their loyal following, I would not have enjoyed thirty-seven years of sharing my passion for cooking and developing these recipes.

I thank Dierbergs School of Cooking for the opportunity to teach, for their assistance making the classes run smoothly, and for their support of this cookbook project. I have also enjoyed the privilege of styling the food for Dierbergs *Everybody Cooks®* magazine and TV show series.

This book is a collection of recipes, but the recipes might still be filed away in notebooks if it were not for the assistance, mentoring, and encouragement of many people. I am indebted to Gena Bast who has provided professional technical advice and has been my editor, entering the material into electronic media for publishing, writing copy, editing, advising, and always encouraging me. Janice Martin and Patty Tomaselli helped ensure that the recipes were written accurately and consistently to help even the novice cook. Carol Hollenbeck has the keenest eyes of anyone I know and has been an invaluable lead proofreader and adviser. Thanks to Cathy Davis of *Davis Creative* and Tim Hill for their publishing mentoring and to Barb Ostmann for her culinary advice. Eszter Clark's cover and interior design and Steve Adams' photography have resulted in a beautiful cookbook of which I am very proud.

I would be remiss not to thank longtime friends Milt and Diane Blood, Rod and Carol Hollenbeck, Mike and Sandy King, Ed and Hanne Knierim, Paul and Leslie Markovits, and Bob and Cathy Putz for being willing and constructive tasters, advisers, and supporters of my culinary endeavors. Thanks also to my extended family and especially to my sister, Ardell, who has always been my inspiration and teammate.

As much as I enjoy cooking for others, my true joy is cooking for my husband, Lyle, our sons Mike and Matt, and our daughter-in-law, Abbie. Mike and Matt are proud of their mother's cooking, and I am so proud of them as my sons. And the person I am most thankful for is my wonderful husband who has been at my side for over forty years. His patience, understanding, and helpfulness were invaluable on this project and I have always appreciated his ability to be spot-on in his evaluation of the food I have prepared.

I love you all!

Table of Contents

My
Story

Teaching cooking classes and styling food for photography is intriguing to some people. What sprouted my interest and how food became a career are questions I am frequently asked. I think I was born into it. There was no better school for teaching me about food than my family's farm in southern Minnesota.

My family produced nearly all of our food. We raised, harvested, preserved, cooked and ate it. Only staples like baking supplies and breakfast cereal were purchased from the grocery store. We had fresh milk, beef, pork, poultry and eggs. Homemade sausage was cured in a stone smokehouse. Enough potatoes were raised to fill two large bins in the cellar. My mother had a huge garden. Whatever wasn't eaten immediately was frozen or canned for later use. Strawberries and raspberries seemed to need picking all summer long. Apples were abundant in the fall.

Food styling the Lemon Blueberry Trifle at Steve Adams Studio in St. Louis, 2013.

As the youngest of four, life was pretty easy as far as doing farm work, and I was able to help my mother with cooking and food preparation. Meat, potatoes and gravy, fresh vegetables and a homemade dessert were standard fare during that time, but not every family's meals were as tasty as my mother's. She knew how to make food taste delicious and liked to make food special when entertaining. She shared those genes with me and taught me the basics.

At age nine, I was finally old enough to become a 4H Club member, and thus began my food career. In 4H Club, we had projects. My favorites were food preparation and bread baking. The club leaders inspired us to do our best in whatever we were doing. I learned the fundamentals of making good cakes, pies, cookies, and breads, and made them for the annual county fair competitions hoping they would win blue ribbons. We also gave

I have great childhood memories of growing up on our farm in Minnesota.

demonstrations. My favorite topics were food-related. It was through these demonstrations that I learned to cook and talk at the same time, to be organized, and to teach.

The first eighteen years of my life established my food roots, and there were a few *ah-ha* moments when I realized food is more than just something to sustain us. One of my earliest recollections of food (other than my mother's), was that of Spam® baked with canned peaches and a generous topping of brown sugar, made by an elderly aunt. I never had anything like that, and I still remember the contrasting sweet and salty flavor and the crunchy caramelized crust. Another new food experience, both socially and sensory, was eating succulent steamed crabs piled on a newspaper-covered picnic table in the backyard of my host family while on a 4H Club trip to Maryland. That was a unique experience for a Midwestern girl who had never traveled more than 200 miles from home. I could write pages about new food discoveries which are still vivid in my mind, still some of the most memorable moments in my life.

After graduating from the University of Minnesota with a Bachelor of Science degree in foods and business, I first worked in the test kitchen of Meredith Publishing® Company in Des Moines, Iowa, testing recipes for *Better Homes & Gardens®* magazines and cookbooks. This surpassed my dreams. I was introduced to foods even more exciting than Spam® and steamed crab! I learned

how to test and develop recipes and began to gain experience styling food. It was during this period of time that the gastronomic revolution in America spearheaded by Julia Child erupted. Food in homes was moving beyond meat, potatoes, and TV dinners. Restaurants were introducing new foods and menus. Cooking classes and television shows were the rage. Cookbooks appeared overnight on bookshelves. It was an exciting time to be working in the culinary world!

An opportunity to work in the refrigerated products consumer services department of The Pillsbury® Company brought me back to Minneapolis. My job there included baking many 'canned' biscuits and crescent rolls for recipe development, consumer testing, photography for package labels and TV commercials. One highlight of my work there was researching scratch biscuits in the South. This led to the development of a new Pillsbury product.

Working in the Pillsbury® test kitchen, making cinnamon rolls, in the 1970s.

Another highlight was supervising the testing and selecting of the 100 finalist recipes for the 1972 Bake-Off® in Beverly Hills, California.

When my husband took a job in St. Louis, a new culinary chapter in my life began. An impromptu visit to the Pampered Pantry Kitchen Store and Cooking School turned into a job as manager of the cooking school and the beginning of thirty-seven years teaching cooking classes. It was only natural that the first classes would be bread baking, then a hot topic. Microwave cooking

With The Pampered Pantry team in the mid 1970s. From left to right: Marie Mosher, Tony Bommarito, Susan Katzman, Jean-Pierre Augé, Carol Ziemann, Andre Gotti, and Eli Strassner

was another very popular subject and consumers were eager to learn how to use that magic appliance. There were waiting lists for my classes which, according to Helen McCully, food editor of *House Beautiful,* were the first to be taught in a cooking school rather than by an oven distributor. Another new appliance at that time was the consumer food processor. The Pampered Pantry was the exclusive store In the St. Louis area to sell Cusinart® food processors. The first food processors used in my classes were test models. Bread baking, microwave, and food processor classes expanded into other class topics. Through the Pampered Pantry, I was hired to prepare and arrange food for a local photographer. This led to a new career in food styling and recipe development for advertising, packaging, and publications.

With sons Matt (left) and Mike (right) in 1981. They were so eager to taste my freshly made Cherry Cheese Stollen (page 93).

The Dierbergs Everybody Cooks© team in 2013 with Tyler Florence. From left to right: Trish Farano, Janice Martin, Marianne Moore, Tyler Florence, Barb Ridenhour, Carol Ziemann, Patty Tomaselli, and Therese Lewis

In 1978, Dierbergs Markets in St. Louis opened the first cooking school in a supermarket in the country. I was recruited to teach one month after the school opened. Class topics ran the gamut from bread baking and microwave cooking to all about apples, but the most popular classes by far were "Summer Patio Buffet" for casual entertaining and "A Country Inn Christmas" for holiday entertaining. Each year, I created new menus and the classes had loyal followings. Because many students often requested that I create a cookbook, I finally took a break from teaching to write this book which is a collection of favorite recipes of students, friends, and family. I hope you enjoy this book and find many new favorites to add to your collection.

Happy cooking and eating!

Carol

Getting Started...

Before every cooking class, set-up notes to the cooking school identified special ingredients, ingredient preparation, and cooking equipment that would be used during class to insure the recipes would be just as I expected. Following are set-up notes to help you make these recipes just as expected.

Butter   I usually use real butter when cooking and I always use unsalted butter unless otherwise specified. Unsalted butter keeps the salt level neutral for adding other seasonings. Margarine can be substituted in many recipes, but it should always be 80% fat. For best results, always use butter for baking.

Room Temp versus Softened   Ingredients, especially butter, cream cheese, and eggs, should be room temperature for best volume and texture in baked goods. Place ingredients on the counter for 20 to 30 minutes before using. Room temperature consistency is perfect when butter holds its shape and a press of the thumb leaves an imprint. If butter can be stirred, it is too soft for best baking results but is perfect for adding additional ingredients as for flavored butters or appetizer spreads. Warm the butter or cream cheese at room temperature up to 1 hour or microwave on 20% power just until softened.

Oils   All oils have the same number of calories, but may have a different flavor and fat composition. I use canola vegetable oil for general purpose cooking. I use extra virgin olive oil when I want a fruity, olive flavor. Plain olive oil has a less pronounced flavor. Light olive oil has the same amount of fat but is very refined and has little flavor.

Flour   Use all-purpose bleached or unbleached flour unless otherwise specified. Stir the flour before spooning it into a measuring cup and leveling with a knife.

Eggs   Use large eggs and always use pasteurized eggs if they will be eaten without thoroughly cooking.

Salt   I use coarse salt, either kosher or sea salt, for the flavor and texture sprinkling on salads, meats, and vegetables. Fine-textured common table salt is used for baking because it blends better with dry ingredients.

Pepper   Freshly ground black pepper is used unless otherwise specified. I love the disposable grinders which adjust from fine to coarse consistency.

Broths versus Stocks   Broths are liquids made by cooking vegetables, meats, or fish with seasonings in water. Stocks also include meat or fish bones making stocks much more flavorful and a better choice for many soups and sauces. Reduced sodium broths and stocks lower the amount of salt in recipes and allow other flavors to shine through.

Herbs The best way to store most fresh herbs is to treat them like a bouquet of flowers. Remove the lower leaves from the stems, make a fresh stem cut, and stand them upright in a small amount of water in a tall covered container or cover with a plastic bag. Store all herbs, except basil, in the refrigerator. Basil is very sensitive to cold and may turn black. It is best left, uncovered, in a cool spot on the kitchen counter. Harvest herbs from your garden early in the morning when it is cool.

Dried herbs should be stored in a cool, dark place in your kitchen and used within 6 months. Write the date on the label when the jar is opened. Dried herbs are best added to food while it is cooking and fresh herbs are best added at the end of cooking for a fresh burst of flavor.

Salad Greens Even though many salad greens are pre-washed, they can be made more crisp and refreshing by rinsing. I recommend rinsing sturdy greens (spinach, leaf lettuces, arugula), spinning dry, and loosely storing in a covered container or plastic bag with a paper towel to absorb excess moisture in the refrigerator for an hour or two before serving. It is best to just sprinkle delicate greens (mixed baby greens, spring mix) lightly with water before refrigerating.

Garlic One clove garlic, minced, is about 1 teaspoon. Separate cloves by wrapping garlic head in a towel and hitting it with a heavy pan. Separated cloves can be stored in a container in the refrigerator.

Roasted Garlic Using a sharp knife, slice top off garlic bulb to expose top of cloves. Remove any loose outer peel and place bulb on square of foil. Drizzle with 1 tablespoon olive oil. Tightly wrap garlic in foil. Bake in 375°F oven for 45 minutes or until soft. Cool; squeeze cloves to remove pulp.

Roasted Bell Peppers Cut peppers, from top to bottom, into quarters; remove seeds and any membranes. Place peppers, skin side up, on foil-lined baking sheet; press with hand to flatten. Broil close to heat source until charred. Wrap peppers in foil. Cool for 10 to 15 minutes. Remove and discard charred skin.

Ingredient Piece Size

To Chop is to randomly cut food into smaller pieces from ¼ inch to ½ inch.
To Mince is to chop very fine, less than ⅛-inch.
To Cube or Dice is to cut in square pieces. Diced ingredients are ½ inch or less; cubes are larger.
Bite-Size Pieces are about 1-inch but depends on the food.

Commonly Used Saucepans

Small (less than 2 quarts); medium (2 to 3 quarts); large (3 to 4 quarts); Dutch oven (6 quarts or larger)

Commonly Used Skillets

Small (less than 8 inches); medium (8 to 10 inches); large (10 to 12 inches); extra-large (larger than 12 inches)

To my wonderful family . . .
For the joy they bring to my life, for their encouragement and support,
and for their participation as taste-testers throughout my career.

From left to right: Matt, Abbie, Carol, Lyle and Mike.

APPETIZERS

Appetizers and party food don't have to be complicated
to make. From casual to elegant,
these recipes have all received rave reviews.

Herbed Crostini

Crostini means "little toasts" in Italian and are small, thin slices of toasted bread. Many recipes for spreads and dips will suggest serving them on crostini. They can be the base for many bruschetta toppings and crostini also make great croutons for soups and salads. Herbs are optional.

Ingredients

1 French bread baguette
4 tablespoons extra virgin olive oil
1 large clove garlic, minced

1 teaspoon minced fresh or dried oregano or rosemary

Preheat oven to 400°F. Combine olive oil, garlic, and oregano or rosemary in a small bowl. Slice baguette into ¼ to ½-inch-thick slices. Place slices on a parchment-lined baking sheet. Brush with olive oil mixture. Bake 5 to 10 minutes or until lightly golden browned.

Makes 24 crostini

CAROL'S TIDBITS

Light, airy-textured French bread slices will brown faster than dense-textured French bread slices.

Check the bottom of bread slices after 5 minutes of baking. Turn slices over; continue baking if bottom is golden brown and top is still pale.

Sun-Dried Tomato Spread

Looking for a quick and easy appetizer? Try this tasty spread, or the roasted pepper variation, on crackers or crostini!

Ingredients

2 packages (8 ounces each) cream cheese, softened
⅓ cup oil-packed sun-dried tomatoes, drained

3 green onions, sliced
¼ teaspoon dried basil
¼ teaspoon dried oregano
¼ teaspoon dried thyme

Combine all ingredients in a food processor work bowl; process with short pulses until well blended. Store spread in refrigerator up to one week. Serve on crackers or crostini.

Makes 2 cups

CAROL'S TIDBITS

Other herbs, or herb combinations, may be used; just use a range of ¾ to 1 teaspoon total dried herbs or 1½ to 3 teaspoons fresh herbs.

Variation: Substitute ½ cup roasted red bell pepper for the sun-dried tomatoes.

Garlic & Herb Chèvre Crisps

Slice the baguette on the bias to get long, thin slices that will bake into crispy crostini. Great to serve with a salad or a glass of wine and fresh fruit.

Ingredients

¼ cup extra virgin olive oil
1 clove garlic, minced
1 teaspoon minced fresh or dried rosemary
½ teaspoon minced fresh or dried thyme

1 French bread baguette or ciabatta bread loaf
1 package (6 ounces) chèvre cheese, softened

Preheat oven to 400°F. Combine olive oil, garlic, rosemary, and thyme in a small microwave-safe bowl. Microwave on high (100% power) for 30 seconds; let stand 5 minutes.

Slice baguette into ¼-inch-thick slices. Spread slices with cheese; place on a parchment-lined baking sheet. Strain herbs from olive oil; drizzle oil over cheese. Bake 5 to 10 minutes or until edges are just beginning to brown.

Makes 24 to 30 slices

Herbed Caprese Bruschetta

Garden fresh tomatoes and basil star in this simple appetizer. Garlic herb cheese is the surprise twist to a classic caprese bruschetta.

Ingredients

¼ cup extra virgin olive oil
1 clove garlic, minced
1 French bread baguette
1 package (5 to 8 ounces) garlic herb spreadable cream-style cheese

16 to 18 fresh basil leaves
16 to 18 small tomato slices
Coarse salt
Freshly ground black pepper
Reduced balsamic vinegar, if desired

Preheat oven to 400°F. Combine olive oil and garlic in a small bowl. Slice baguette diagonally into ¾-inch-thick slices. Place baguette slices on a parchment-lined baking sheet; brush with olive oil mixture. Bake 5 to 10 minutes or until lightly browned.

Spread baguette slices with garlic herb cheese; top each slice with a basil leaf and tomato slice. Sprinkle with salt and pepper. Drizzle with balsamic vinegar.

Makes 16 to 18 bruschetta

Tapenade Spread

Tapenade is an olive paste with capers and seasonings, often served with crusty bread. Sometimes it is served with cream cheese on crackers or pita chips.

Ingredients

¾ cup pitted ripe olives
½ cup pimiento-stuffed Spanish green olives
1½ tablespoons pine nuts or sunflower seeds
1 tablespoon capers, drained and rinsed

1½ teaspoons chopped fresh parsley
1 clove garlic, minced
1 teaspoon lemon juice
½ teaspoon Italian seasoning
Dash cayenne pepper
1 package (8 ounce) cream cheese, cut into small pieces and softened

Combine all ingredients except cream cheese in a food processor work bowl; process with short pulses for 30 seconds.

Add cream cheese and pulse just until blended. Chill before serving. Garnish with whole or sliced olives. Serve with sliced bread, pita chips or crackers.

Makes 1½ cups spread

Toasted Pita Crisps

Pita bread, cut into triangles and toasted, is an alternative to crostini for spreads and dips. The crisps are a great snack even without a spread or dip.

Ingredients

2 to 3 pita rounds
Extra virgin olive oil
Dried oregano, crushed

Dried basil, crushed
Coarse salt

Preheat oven to 350°F. Separate each pita round into two thin rounds; place on a parchment-lined baking sheet. Brush with olive oil; sprinkle with oregano, basil and salt. Cut pita rounds into 8 triangles. Bake 10 to 12 minutes or until crisp and lightly browned.

Makes 32-48 crisps

CAROL'S TIDBITS

Tapenade hails from Provence, France but is popular all along the Mediterranean coast and is believed to have been eaten in Italy for centuries.

The olive garnish helps identify what it is.

In this recipe, tapenade is blended into cream cheese to make an appetizer that is easier to serve and eat. Omit cream cheese if you prefer to serve plain tapenade.

Italian
Cheese Torte

Softened blocks of gorgonzola or feta cheese will be more creamy than pre-crumbled cheese.

Any 3-cup capacity container may be used for the torte mold. Rinsing the mold with water will help hold the plastic wrap in place when layering the cheese and pesto.

Commercial pesto may be substituted for basil, Parmesan, olive oil, garlic, pine nuts, and salt and pepper, but strain excess oil from the pesto before using or the torte will be too soft. Use the oil on pasta or for a dipping oil for bread.

Because most molds for tortes are tapered, use smaller quantities of cheese and pesto for the first layers to keep layering more uniform.

Most everyone loves cheese and pesto, signature flavors of Italy. Use basil when it is abundant in your garden to make fresh pesto for this layered cheese torte. Enjoy it spread on herbed crostini or crackers.

Ingredients

1 package (8 ounces) gorgonzola or feta cheese, softened
1 package (8 ounces) cream cheese, softened
4 tablespoons butter, softened
1 cup lightly packed fresh basil leaves

⅓ cup grated Parmesan cheese
2 tablespoons extra virgin olive oil
1 clove garlic
2 tablespoons pine nuts, if desired
Salt and pepper

Add gorgonzola or feta cheese to a food processor work bowl; process until smooth. Add cream cheese and butter; process until smooth. Remove mixture from processor bowl and set aside.

Add basil, Parmesan, olive oil, and garlic to the work bowl; process with short pulses until almost paste consistency. Remove processor blade and stir in pine nuts; season with salt and pepper.

Line a 3-cup bowl or loaf pan with plastic wrap or damp cheesecloth. Spread one-fourth of the cheese mixture in an even layer in the pan. Cover with half of the pesto mixture. Repeat layering with half of the remaining cheese mixture, the remaining pesto, and the remaining cheese mixture. Cover torte with plastic wrap; chill at least 2 hours or up to 4 days.

To serve, unmold torte onto a serving platter and let stand at room temperature about 15 minutes. Serve with Herbed Crostini (page 17) or crackers.

Makes 2½ cups spread

Roasted Pepper Caponata

This medley of roasted peppers, tomatoes, and olives is like caponata without eggplant. It is most flavorful when made ahead and served at room temperature with toasted pita crisps or crostini.

Ingredients

1 red bell pepper
1 yellow bell pepper
1 cup sliced onion
2 tablespoons extra virgin olive oil
2 large Roma tomatoes, peeled, seeded, and chopped

2 teaspoons balsamic vinegar
Dash coarse salt
½ cup sliced, pitted kalamata or ripe olives
2 tablespoons chopped fresh basil
½ cup crumbled feta cheese

Preheat broiler. Cut peppers into quarters and remove seeds; place skin-side up on a foil-lined baking sheet. Roast peppers about 4 inches under broiler until skin is blistered and black. Wrap peppers in the foil and let stand for 5 minutes. Remove skin and cut peppers into strips.

Heat olive oil in a medium skillet over medium-high heat. Add onion and cook, stirring occasionally until tender. Stir in peppers, tomatoes, vinegar, and salt; cook until juices have evaporated. Remove skillet from heat; stir in olives and basil. Spread caponata in a shallow serving dish; sprinkle with feta cheese. Serve slightly warm or at room temperature with Toasted Pita Crisps (page 19) or Herbed Crostini (page 17).

Makes 2 cups caponata

CAROL'S TIDBITS

Caponata is a sweet and sour Italian eggplant relish often served with crusty bread or crostini.

Flavor improves if made ahead and refrigerated; warm slightly before serving.

I like to serve along with Italian Cheese Torte (on previous page).

Whidbey Island Smoked Salmon Mousse

CAROL'S TIDBITS

Cold-smoked salmon is smoked at a low temperature which does not cook the salmon. It is usually sold thinly sliced.

Prepared horseradish is grated horseradish preserved in vinegar. Store the jar upside-down in the refrigerator to preserve the fresh flavor and creamy white color.

This wonderful mousse was inspired by an inn on Whidbey Island in the San Juan Islands north of Seattle. It is made with cold-smoked salmon which has a mild flavor and a moist, delicate texture.

Ingredients

4 ounces (½ of an 8-ounce package) cream cheese, softened
¾ teaspoon minced shallot
¾ teaspoon minced fresh parsley
¾ teaspoon chopped fresh chives or dill

¾ teaspoon minced garlic
¾ teaspoon prepared horseradish
½ teaspoon lemon juice
1 package (4 ounces) cold-smoked salmon, coarsely chopped
Pita chips or crostini

Combine all ingredients, except salmon and chips, in a medium bowl; stir until well blended. Add salmon; mix just until salmon is evenly mixed in. Cover and chill for 1 to 2 hours before serving. Serve with pita chips or crostini. It is also very good with crusty bread, or on toasted bagels or English muffins, or as a filling for omelets and quesadillas.

Makes 1½ cups spread

Variation: Hot-smoked salmon may be substituted for cold-smoked salmon. It has a flaky, cooked salmon texture and a mild, smoky flavor. It has the appearance of a salmon fillet when packaged and may be seasoned with herbs and spices.

Crostini with White Bean Hummus, Baked Shiitake Mushrooms, and Roasted Red Peppers

Build this flavorful vegetarian appetizer with crostini and toppings of a mild version of the popular Middle Eastern hummus, crispy baked mushrooms, and roasted peppers.

Ingredients

White Bean Hummus
1 bulb garlic, roasted (page 13)
1 can (15 ounces) cannellini white beans, drained and rinsed
¼ cup olive oil
1 tablespoon fresh lemon juice
½ teaspoon minced fresh rosemary
½ teaspoon coarse salt

Baked Shiitake Mushrooms
8 ounces shiitake mushrooms, stemmed and thinly sliced
¼ cup olive oil
1½ to 2 teaspoons minced fresh rosemary
1½ to 2 teaspoons minced fresh thyme
½ teaspoon coarse ground black pepper
¼ teaspoon coarse salt

Roasted Red Peppers
2 red bell peppers, roasted (page 13)
1 tablespoon extra virgin olive oil

Crostini (page 17) or warm pita bread triangles

For hummus: Combine all hummus ingredients in a food processor work bowl; process until smooth. Transfer to a serving bowl.

For mushrooms: Preheat oven to 400°F. Toss mushrooms with olive oil, rosemary, thyme, pepper, and salt on a rimmed baking sheet. Bake 15 to 20 minutes or until mushrooms are cooked and edges are beginning to crisp. Transfer to a serving bowl.

For peppers: Dice peppers. Place in a serving bowl and drizzle with olive oil.

To serve: Spread hummus on crostini or pita bread triangles. Top with mushrooms and/or peppers.

Makes 30 crostini

CAROL'S TIDBITS

Any white bean can be used to make the hummus, but I prefer cannellini beans which are white Italian kidney beans. They are popular for soups and salads. Navy beans and great Northern beans are commonly used in baked beans. Hummus is traditionally made with chickpeas, also known as garbanzo beans.

Shiitake mushrooms have a rich, steak-like flavor. The stems are tough and usually discarded. Small white button mushrooms have a very mild flavor. Baby bella mushrooms, also known as cremini mushrooms, are immature portabella mushrooms. Their flavor is also mild, but a bit more intense than white button mushrooms and have a firmer texture. These mushrooms may be substituted for part of the shiitake mushrooms.

Three Pepper
Quesadillas

CAROL'S TIDBITS

To make ahead, prepare as directed; cover tightly and refrigerate until ready to brown. Heating time may be slightly longer to melt the cheese.

Quesadillas may be cooked in a skillet over medium heat until browned and crisp, about 1 to 2 minutes per side.

These quesadillas are never on the platter very long whenever I make them. The creamy, melted cheese complements the slightly crunchy peppers flavored with cumin. I also serve these as a grilled cheese sandwich.

Ingredients

4 tablespoons butter
1 thinly sliced green bell pepper
(about 1½ cups)
1 thinly sliced red bell pepper
(about 1½ cups)
1 thinly sliced yellow bell pepper
(about 1½ cups)
1 cup thinly sliced onion

1 teaspoon ground cumin
1 package (8 ounces) cream cheese, softened
2 cups (8 ounces) shredded sharp Cheddar cheese
½ cup grated Parmesan cheese
10 (8-inch) flour tortillas
Salsa

Melt the butter in a large skillet over medium-high heat. Add peppers and onion; cook stirring occasionally until tender. Stir in cumin. Drain peppers, reserving liquid; set both aside.

Preheat oven to 425°F. Combine the three cheeses in the bowl of an electric mixer and beat until fluffy. Spread 2 tablespoons of the cheese mixture over each tortilla. Spoon pepper mixture over half of each tortilla; fold tortillas in half.

Place quesadillas on a parchment-lined baking sheet. Brush both sides with the reserved liquid. Bake 10 to 12 minutes or until lightly browned. Cool slightly before cutting each quesadilla into 3 wedges. Serve warm with salsa.

Makes 30 wedges

Caramelized Onion and Goat Cheese Quesadillas

Sweet caramelized onions and the delightfully tart flavor of goat cheese are an unexpected surprise in quesadillas. I would pass on the margarita and enjoy these with a glass of red wine.

Ingredients

1 tablespoon olive oil
2 cups slivered onion
Coarse salt
6 (8-inch) flour tortillas
1 package (6 ounces) goat cheese
   with herbs or garlic

Olive oil
Dairy sour cream, if desired
Reduced balsamic vinegar, if desired

Heat a large skillet over medium heat. Add olive oil and onion; sprinkle with salt. Cover skillet and cook until onions begin to wilt. Remove cover and cook onions, stirring frequently, until onions are golden brown (reduce heat if onions cook too quickly). Set aside to cool slightly.

Spread about 2 tablespoons goat cheese over each tortilla. Spoon onions onto one half of each tortilla; fold tortilla in half. Brush tortillas with olive oil. Cook 2 folded quesadillas at a time in a 10-inch skillet over medium heat until bottom side is browned, about 2 minutes. Turn tortillas over and cook until browned on second side. Cool slightly and cut each quesadilla into 3 wedges. Serve with sour cream and a drizzle of balsamic vinegar.

Makes 18 wedges

Variation: Substitute 2 red or yellow bell peppers, quartered, seeded and cut crosswise into thin strips for the onion. Cook until tender and beginning to brown.

CAROL'S TIDBITS

Cook quesadillas on griddle or grill pan if cooking a quantity of quesadillas at a time.

Prepared quesadillas may also be placed on a baking sheet and baked in a 425°F oven for 8 to 10 minutes, or placed on grid over medium-high coals and grilled about 2 minutes per side.

Use no-stick cooking spray as alternative to olive oil.

Black Bean Confetti Salsa

CAROL'S TIDBITS

Slip your hand into a small plastic bag to hold the jalepeño pepper when removing the seeds and chopping.

Combine salsa and Mexican queso or Monterey Jack cheese for a quesadilla filling.

Combine with rice for a burrito filling.

Although great with corn chips, don't limit yourself to serving this salsa with chips only. It is a wonderful salsa with grilled pork and chicken.

Ingredients

1 can (15 ounces) black beans, drained and rinsed
1 can (11 ounces) vacuum-packed corn, drained
½ cup diced red bell pepper
¼ cup diced red onion

1 jalapeño pepper, finely chopped
2 tablespoons white vinegar
1 tablespoon olive oil
1 teaspoon ground cumin
½ teaspoon chili powder
½ teaspoon cayenne pepper

Combine all ingredients in a medium bowl. Chill at least 1 hour before serving.

Makes 3½ cups

Margarita Fruit Salsa

CAROL'S TIDBITS

Other fresh fruits may be used, but the mango and strawberry combination seems especially good. The kiwi adds color more than flavor.

Serve with lime tortilla chips or with grilled chicken or fish.

Cointreau and Triple Sec are orange-flavored liqueurs.

Rim a margarita glass with course salt or sugar and fill with this refreshing fruit salsa. Surround the glass with tortilla chips; add a fresh lime garnish.

Ingredients

1 container (8 ounces) fresh strawberries, diced
4 to 5 slices fresh pineapple, diced
2 kiwi, peeled and diced
1 mango, peeled, seeded and diced
2 tablespoons sugar

1 teaspoon grated lime peel
2 tablespoons fresh lime juice
1½ tablespoons tequila
1½ tablespoons orange-flavored liqueur

Combine strawberries, pineapple, kiwi, and mango in a large bowl. Combine sugar, lime peel and juice, tequila, and orange liqueur in a 1-cup measure. Pour over fruit and stir gently. Chill for 1 to 2 hours before serving.

Makes 4 cups salsa

Savory Spanakopita Bites

Spiraled puff pastry slices are filled with the flavors of Greece...spinach, red peppers, olive oil, and feta. This appetizer will remind you of the classic spanakopita pie.

Ingredients

1 sheet (½ of 17.3-ounce box) frozen puff pastry

1 tablespoon olive oil

½ cup sliced green onion

½ cup diced red bell pepper

1 package (10 ounces) frozen chopped spinach, thawed and well-drained

1¼ cups (5 ounces) crumbled feta cheese

1 tablespoon fresh lemon juice

¼ teaspoon freshly grated nutmeg

Coarse salt

Freshly ground black pepper

1 egg, separated

Thaw puff pastry at room temperature according to package directions.

Heat olive oil in a small skillet over medium heat. Stir in onion and pepper; cook until tender. Transfer to a medium bowl and cool. Stir in spinach, feta, lemon juice, and nutmeg; season with salt and pepper. Stir in egg yolk (reserve white for glaze); set aside.

Preheat oven to 400°F. Roll pastry into a 13-inch square on a lightly floured surface. Cut pastry in half to form two rectangles. Spread half of the spinach filling over each rectangle leaving 1-inch border on all sides. Brush edges of pastry with egg white beaten with 1 tablespoon water. Starting at one long side, loosely roll up each pastry jellyroll-style; press edges firmly to seal. Place pastries on a parchment-lined baking sheet. Using a sharp knife, cut score lines crosswise in top of pastries, spacing about ¾-inch apart. Brush pastries with egg white mixture. Bake 25 to 30 minutes or until lightly browned. Cool about 10 minutes before cutting into slices.

Makes about 30 slices

Mini Mushroom Tarts

CAROL'S TIDBITS

Chop mushrooms until pieces are about ¼ inch in size.

Try a variety of mushrooms for different flavors. Chop both caps and stems of most mushrooms; discard woody shiitake stems.

Spoon sour cream for garnish into a small plastic bag. Snip off one corner to make a small hole; squeeze sour cream onto baked tarts.

Guests will love these scrumptious little mushroom tarts that taste like baked mushrooms; you will love that they are so much easier and faster to make. Fill the mini shells ahead and refrigerate until ready to pop into the oven when guests arrive.

Ingredients

1 tablespoon butter
3 cups (10 ounces) chopped
  mushrooms
2 tablespoons chopped shallot
¼ teaspoon coarse salt
¼ teaspoon curry powder
2 tablespoons dry sherry

¼ cup dairy sour cream
1 tablespoon dry bread crumbs
1 box (1.9 ounces) frozen mini fillo
  shells, thawed
Dairy sour cream for garnish
Chopped fresh parsley

Preheat oven to 350°F. Melt butter in a medium skillet over medium-high heat. Stir in mushrooms, shallot, salt, curry powder, and dry sherry; cook stirring often until all liquid has evaporated. Cool. Stir in the ¼ cup sour cream.

Fill fillo shells with mushroom filling, about 1 tablespoon per shell; place on a baking sheet. Bake 10 to 12 minutes or until shells are lightly browned.

Serve warm with a dollop of sour cream and a sprinkle of chopped parsley.

Makes 15 mini tarts

Grilled Prosciutto-Wrapped Asparagus Spears

Elegant and impressive in appearance and taste, this is one of my top choices to serve for a special occasion. The salty prosciutto, the mild asparagus, and the zippy mustard sauce are the perfect combination to serve at a champagne event. See photo on page16.

Ingredients

⅓ cup mayonnaise
⅓ cup dairy sour cream
2 tablespoons Dijon mustard
1 tablespoon milk

12 large asparagus spears
6 thin slices (about 3 ounces)
   prosciutto, cut in half lengthwise
Olive oil

Combine mayonnaise, sour cream, mustard, and milk in a small bowl; blend until smooth. Chill.

Preheat grill to medium-high. Remove woody ends from asparagus spears; rinse spears and pat dry. Wrap each spear with a strip of prosciutto beginning under the scaled tip and spiral downward toward the cut end. Lightly brush with olive oil.

Place spears diagonally on the grill grid; grill turning occasionally until lightly browned, about 4 to 6 minutes. Serve with Dijon mustard sauce.

Makes 12 spears (4 to 6 servings)

Manchego Cheese Tomato Tart

CAROL'S TIDBITS

Manchego is a hard cheese made only of sheep's milk of the Manchego breed in the La Mancha region of Spain. Its rind has a very recognizable herringbone basket weave pattern.

It has a nutty, slightly sweet flavor and is very smooth when melted. As the cheese ages, its flavor intensifies and becomes sharper, the color becomes more golden, and the texture more crumbly.

Serve Manchego cheese with crusty bread and a glass of wine or sherry or for dessert with fruit.

See page 20 for a basil pesto recipe.

Rich and delicious, popular Manchego cheese stars in this basil and tomato tart inspired by a dinner on the Mediterranean coast of Spain near Marbella.

Ingredients

1 refrigerated pie crust
  (½ of 15-ounce package)
6 tablespoons basil pesto sauce
¾ cup sliced grape tomatoes
6 ounces Manchego cheese, shredded
  (1½ cups)

2 eggs
About ½ cup heavy whipping
  cream
Grated Parmesan cheese
2 cups arugula, if desired
Extra virgin olive oil, if desired

Press pie crust onto bottom and up sides of a 9-inch tart pan with removable bottom; trim off excess dough. Pierce bottom of crust with fork. Chill crust for 30 minutes before baking.

Preheat oven to 375°F. Line the crust with square of foil, pressing it firmly against sides. Bake crust on lower oven shelf for 10 minutes. Remove foil and bake until crust is dry and lightly browned, about 5 to 8 additional minutes. Cool on a wire rack for 5 minutes.

Drain excess oil from pesto; spread pesto over bottom of crust and scatter tomatoes over pesto. Top with shredded cheese. Beat eggs in a 2-cup glass measure; blend in enough cream to make 1 cup custard. Pour custard over cheese; sprinkle with Parmesan.

Place tart on a foil sheet and bake 20 to 25 minutes or until lightly browned and knife inserted near center comes out clean. Cool on a wire rack for 5 minutes before serving.

Serve tart topped with arugula and lightly drizzled with olive oil.

Makes 8 to 10 servings

Note: Recipe may be made in six individual 4-inch tart pans. Two refrigerated crusts will be needed to line the tart pans. Divide remaining ingredients among the six tarts and bake as directed above.

Southern Shrimp and Grits

Shrimp and Grits are a very popular Southern entrée and special occasion appetizer. To some of my St. Louis students, the thought of grits was not very appealing until they tasted this dish. They loved it!

Ingredients

Grits
2 cups (16 ounces) chicken broth
1 cup corn or hominy grits
   (not instant)
2 cups milk
½ teaspoon coarse salt
Dash ground white pepper

Dash cayenne pepper
Freshly grated nutmeg
1 cup (4 ounces) shredded white
   Cheddar cheese
½ cup (2 ounces) shredded
   Parmesan
Heavy whipping cream, if desired

Shrimp
6 slices bacon, diced
1 tablespoon butter
2 cups sliced mushrooms
1 cup sliced green onions
1 clove garlic, minced
1 to 1¼ pounds shrimp, peeled and
   deveined

½ cup (4 ounces) chicken broth
1 tablespoon lemon juice
Hot pepper sauce
Salt and pepper

Bring the 2 cups broth for the grits to a boil in a large saucepan over high heat. Whisk in grits, milk, and salt; cook stirring constantly until mixture bubbles. Reduce heat; cover and simmer. Stir frequently, until liquid is absorbed and grits become soft, about 15 to 20 minutes. Stir in peppers and nutmeg; keep warm over low heat.

Cook bacon in a large skillet over medium heat until crisp. Remove bacon with a slotted spoon to paper towels; set aside. Add butter to drippings in skillet and stir in mushrooms, onions, and garlic; cook over medium heat until mushrooms are tender. Stir in shrimp, the ½ cup broth, and lemon juice; cook just until shrimp turn pink. Season shrimp with hot pepper sauce, salt, and pepper.

Stir cheese into grits. For a rich, creamy consistency, stir in a small amount of cream. Spoon grits into serving bowls; top with shrimp and reserved bacon.

Makes 16 appetizer, or 8 first course, or 4 entrée servings

CAROL'S TIDBITS

Grits refers to any coarsely ground grain, but we are most familiar with white corn grits. Only the inner portion of the corn kernel is used to make hominy grits. Yellow corn is used to make polenta. Coarser ground grits, sometimes referred to as stone ground, are preferred in this recipe as compared to instant grits which are very finely ground.

Medium (43-50 count), large (26 to 30 count), or extra-large (16 to 20 count) shrimp may be used. I tend to use medium shrimp if serving as an appetizer and large or extra-large shrimp if serving as an entrée.

Heartland Crab Cakes

CAROL'S TIDBITS

Substitute Old Bay Seasoning for the chili powder and cumin if you want a more traditional Chesapeake Bay crab cake flavor.

Claw crabmeat is the least expensive, most intensely flavored, and best used in highly seasoned dishes. Colossal lump crabmeat is the most expensive crabmeat, best reserved for very special, mildly seasoned dishes. White, backfin, and plain lump crabmeat are perfect for crab cakes.

Juicy, locally grown tomatoes in the Sweet Tomato Sauce and seasonings of the southwest give these crab cakes a heartland twist.

Ingredients

Sweet Tomato Sauce

3 medium tomatoes, peeled, seeded, and chopped (about 3 cups)
⅓ cup water
1 tablespoon brown sugar

1 tablespoon snipped fresh cilantro
1 tablespoon fresh lemon juice
¼ cup vegetable oil
Salt and pepper

Crab Cakes

6.5 to 8 ounces refrigerated white or lump crab meat
⅓ cup mayonnaise
¼ cup finely chopped red bell pepper
2 tablespoons finely chopped green onion or shallot
1 clove garlic, minced

1 teaspoon chili powder
½ teaspoon ground cumin
¼ teaspoon salt
¼ teaspoon black pepper
2 cups soft fresh bread crumbs, divided
2 tablespoons vegetable oil

For sauce: Combine tomatoes, water, and brown sugar in a small saucepan; bring to a boil over high heat. Reduce heat and simmer, uncovered, for 15 to 20 minutes until mixture is reduced by half. Remove from heat and cool.

Place tomato mixture, cilantro, and lemon juice in a blender container; process until well blended. With blender running, slowly add oil in a steady stream; process until well blended. Season with salt and pepper; set aside.

For crab cakes: Drain, lightly rinse, and flake crab meat. Combine mayonnaise, bell pepper, onion, garlic, chili powder, cumin, salt, and pepper in a medium bowl. Stir in crab meat and 1 cup of the bread crumbs; mix well. Spread remaining crumbs on a sheet of wax paper. Shape mixture into 8 balls; roll in remaining bread crumbs and flatten into patties. Chill patties for 30 minutes.

Heat oil in a large skillet over medium-high heat. Cook crab cakes over medium-high heat for 3 to 4 minutes on each side or until golden and heated through. Remove crab cakes and drain on paper towels. Serve with Sweet Tomato Sauce.

Makes 8 crab cakes and 1 cup sauce

Thai Chicken Lettuce Wraps

Lettuce wraps are a hands-required appetizer best served sitting around a table with friends enjoying the good food and conversation.

Ingredients

2 tablespoons dark sesame oil

1 pound boneless, skinless chicken breast halves, diced

1 package (8 ounces) fresh mushrooms, diced

1 red bell pepper, diced

½ cup sliced green onions

2 large cloves garlic, minced

⅔ cup unsweetened coconut milk

2 tablespoons hoisin sauce

1 tablespoon minced fresh ginger

¼ teaspoon salt

Cayenne pepper or crushed red pepper flakes

½ cup lightly salted peanuts, chopped

Chopped cilantro, if desired

1 medium head napa cabbage

Heat a wok or large skillet over high heat. Add sesame oil and chicken; stir-fry until lightly browned. Stir in mushrooms, bell pepper, onions, and garlic; stir-fry until liquid is evaporated. Stir in coconut milk, hoison sauce, ginger, salt, and cayenne pepper to taste; stir-fry until sauce is thickened. Spoon into a serving dish; sprinkle with peanuts and cilantro.

Separate cabbage into leaves and trim top 4 to 5 inches from each leaf to use for lettuce cups (use remainder of leaf in salads, stir-fries, or egg rolls). To serve, spoon a generous tablespoon of chicken mixture in center of leaf; fold tip of leaf over chicken and then fold leaf in half like a taco.

Makes about 16 servings

CAROL'S TIDBITS

Look for unsweetened coconut milk in the Asian section of the grocery store. Do not confuse it with sweetened cream of coconut used to make piña coladas.

The best way to peel fresh ginger is to rub the skin off with the side of a teaspoon. Wrap unused ginger in foil and store in the freezer. It takes only a few minutes for it to thaw enough to grate or chop.

Crispy iceberg lettuce is most often used in lettuce wraps. Napa cabbage, also known as Chinese cabbage, has long, thin, crinkly leaves which make it easy for folding around the filling. I like its mild, delicate flavor. Bibb lettuce is softer and another good wrap alternative.

Swedish Meatballs With Lingonberries

CAROL'S TIDBITS

Meatloaf mix is a mixture of equal parts beef, pork, and veal. If the mix is unavailable, get ⅓ to ½ pounds of each of the meats and make your own mixture. Veal makes the meatballs especially tender and flavorful.

The usual rule is to not over-mix meat or it will be tough. In this instance, using a mixer to beat the mixture actually gives the meatballs a very fine, delicate texture.

Use a #40 ice cream scoop, about 2 tablespoons, to measure meat mixture for shaping. Shape mixture with wet hands or wear vinyl gloves to keep meat from sticking to your hands.

In spite of growing up in Swedish Minnesota, it took a trip to Sweden to fall in love with Swedish meatballs. They are now frequently served at our house as an appetizer in a creamy lingonberry sauce or as an entrée in a more traditional sauce with mashed potatoes on the side.

Ingredients

1 tablespoon olive oil
½ cup finely minced onion
⅓ cup fine dry bread crumbs
⅓ cup milk
1⅓ pounds meatloaf mix
1 egg

1 teaspoon salt
½ teaspoon freshly grated nutmeg
¼ teaspoon ground black pepper
Lingonberry or Traditional Swedish
  Meatball Sauce, if desired
Lingonberry preserves

Heat olive oil in a large skillet over medium heat. Add onion and cook stirring often until softened, about 5 minutes; remove from heat to cool. Combine bread crumbs and milk in a small bowl, stirring with a fork until all crumbs are moistened; set aside.

Combine onion, meatloaf mix, egg, salt, nutmeg, and pepper in a large mixer bowl; beat at medium-high speed until smooth, about 1 minute. Add crumb mixture and beat until well blended, about 1 minute.

Preheat oven to 400°F. Line a rimmed baking sheet with foil and coat with no-stick cooking spray.

Shape mixture into meatballs the size of golf balls. Place meatballs on prepared baking sheet; bake 15 minutes. Turn meatballs; bake 7 to 10 additional minutes or until lightly browned. Let meatballs rest about 2 minutes before removing from the baking sheet with a slotted spoon.

Serve in Lingonberry Swedish Meatball Sauce or Traditional Swedish Meatball Sauce (on following page) with additional lingonberry preserves on the side.

Makes 20 to 24 meatballs

Lingonberry Swedish Meatball Sauce

This Lingonberry Sauce is a creamy glaze with a mild sweet-tart fruit flavor.

Ingredients

1 cup (8 ounces) chicken stock
½ cup heavy whipping cream

¼ cup lingonberry preserves

Combine chicken stock, cream, and lingonberry preserves in a large skillet over medium-high heat; bring just to a boil. Reduce heat and simmer 5 minutes. Add baked meatballs to sauce and cook, stirring frequently, until sauce thickens and glazes meatballs, about 10 minutes.

Traditional Swedish Meatball Sauce

This Traditional Sauce is a savory gravy that also tastes great with Planked Potatoes.

Ingredients

3 tablespoons butter
3 tablespoons flour
2 cups (16 ounces) beef stock

¼ cup heavy whipping cream or
  dairy sour cream
Salt and pepper to taste

Melt butter in a small saucepan over medium heat; stir in flour and cook stirring constantly until mixture bubbles. Stir in beef stock; cook stirring often until thickened. Stir in cream; cook stirring frequently over low heat for 5 minutes. Season with salt and pepper. Serve sauce over meatballs or simmer meatballs in the sauce until heated through.

Makes 2 cups sauce

CAROL'S TIDBITS

Lingonberries are smaller, sweeter, and tenderer than cranberries. They are native to Scandinavia and sold as preserves in this country. Look for it in the specialty jam section of the grocery store or where imported food products are sold. Cranberry sauce can be substituted for lingonberry preserves.

For the boldest and best overall flavor, be sure to use stock (not broth) in either sauce.

Planked Potatoes (page 141) are mashed potatoes browned in the oven.

Caramel
Corn

CAROL'S TIDBITS

For a more intense caramel flavor, use all brown sugar; for a light buttery flavor, use all granulated sugar.

Choose natural or light popcorn if using microwave popcorn.

Margarine may cause caramel syrup to separate during cooking and make popcorn sugary.

This caramel corn is a must at our house at Christmas. Be warned, it is very addictive! It ships well and is frequently sent to a friend in New York. It has been sent as far away as Iraq.

Ingredients

5 to 6 quarts popped popcorn
2 cups pecan halves, if desired
1 cup (2 sticks) butter (not margarine)
1 cup granulated sugar
1 cup firmly packed brown sugar

½ teaspoon salt
¼ teaspoon cream of tartar
½ cup light corn syrup
½ teaspoon baking soda

Preheat oven to 275°F. Place popcorn (without any unpopped kernels) and pecans in a large roasting pan coated with no-stick cooking spray. Keep warm in oven while preparing syrup.

Combine butter, sugars, salt, cream of tartar, and corn syrup in a medium saucepan over medium-high heat stirring well; bring to a boil. Boil 5 minutes without stirring.

Remove from heat and stir in baking soda (mixture will bubble up and become foamy). Pour syrup over popcorn and gently toss to coat. Bake 15 minutes; stir. Bake 15 to 20 additional minutes or until syrup coating is crispy. (Best way to check for doneness is to remove a few kernels of popcorn and let cool. If undercooked, popcorn will be sticky; overcooked popcorn will be sugary.) Spread popcorn on parchment paper to cool.

Makes 6 quarts

Palmetto Pecans

Spiced pecans are a great cocktail-party nibbler. Also add them to salads instead of croutons. These pecans have a bit of salt, a bit of sweet, and a bit of spicy heat.

Ingredients

2 tablespoons butter	1½ teaspoons chili powder
3 cups (about 12 ounces) pecan halves	½ teaspoon coarse salt
¼ cup sugar	¼ teaspoon cayenne pepper

Melt butter in a medium skillet (preferably not nonstick) over medium-low heat. Add pecans and cook stirring often until golden brown and fragrant, about 10 to 15 minutes.

Combine sugar, chili powder, salt, and cayenne in a small bowl; add to pecans and stir until pieces are well coated and sugar is just beginning to melt.

Turn pecans out onto parchment paper. Serve warm or at room temperature. Store pecans in an airtight container.

Makes 3 cups pecans

Spicy Cajun Pecans

Prepare as above substituting 2 teaspoons Cajun or Creole seasoning and 2 teaspoons ground cumin for the chili powder and salt.

CAROL'S TIDBITS

Chili powders have a wide variety of flavors and strength so adjust amount according to personal taste preference. I prefer the darker chili powders.

Skillets with nonstick coatings do not allow the sugar to coat the pecans properly.

The inspiration for this particular recipe came from South Carolina, known as the Palmetto State, hence the name Palmetto Pecans.

Old-Fashioned Lemonade

CAROL'S TIDBITS

For individual servings, combine syrup and juice. Use 1 part syrup mixture to 3 parts water.

Increase juice for a more tart lemonade; use more syrup for a sweeter lemonade.

For a sparkling version of lemonade, substitute club soda or a sparkling wine for the water.

To make berry lemonade: Add 1 cup mashed berries when cooking the sugar and water syrup. Strain berries from cooled syrup before using.

There is no match for lemonade made with freshly squeezed lemon juice. It evokes nostalgic memories of the one-room elementary school I attended and the picnics signaling the beginning of summer. Each family brought a jar of sweetened lemon juice and sliced lemons to contribute to the lemonade.

Ingredients

2 cups sugar
11 cups water, divided
1 cup freshly squeezed lemon juice

Lemon slices
Mint leaves

Combine sugar and 2 cups of the water in a small saucepan; heat over medium heat stirring until sugar dissolves. Refrigerate syrup until chilled. Combine syrup, lemon juice, and remaining water in a large pitcher. Serve over ice cubes and garnish with lemon slices and mint leaves.

Makes 3 quarts

Lone Star Peach Sangria

Succulent frozen grapes and peach slices replace ice cubes to keep the sangría from getting diluted. My thanks to Brittany, our nephew's wife, for sharing this recipe with our family.

Ingredients

About 30 green grapes
1 bottle (750 ml) Chardonnay wine
¾ cup peach schnapps or peach brandy
6 tablespoons frozen lemonade concentrate

¼ cup sugar
8 ounces (½ of a 16-ounce package) frozen sliced peaches
10 to 15 large strawberries, halved

Freeze grapes in a single layer on a parchment-lined tray for at least 2 hours.

Combine wine, peach schnapps, lemonade concentrate, and sugar in a pitcher; stir until sugar dissolves. Chill before serving.

To serve, garnish sangría in the pitcher with a few grapes, frozen peach slices, and strawberry halves. Divide remaining fruit among 4 to 6 large wine glasses; fill with sangría. Enjoy!

Makes 4 to 6 servings

CAROL'S TIDBITS

Traditional Spanish sangría is made with red wine, fruit, and sometimes liqueurs or brandy. Sangría blanco is made with white wine. Both are very refreshing served over ice on a hot summer day.

The peach schnapps in this recipe makes this sangria pretty smooth.

Piña Colada Slush

CAROL'S TIDBITS

Piña colada means strained pineapple and is the official drink of Puerto Rico.

Cream of coconut is a thick, sweet mixture of coconut water, and sugar. Stir well before using.

Think sitting poolside or on a warm sunny beach. What could be more refreshing than a tall, frosty piña colada? Keep a container of the slush in the freezer and be ready for an impromptu party.

Ingredients

1 can (46 ounces) pineapple juice
1 can (15 ounces) cream of coconut
2 cups light rum
Carbonated lemon-lime soda, chilled

Pineapple spears for garnish, if desired
Maraschino cherries for garnish, if desired

Combine juice, cream of coconut, and rum in a 3-quart container with a lid. Blend well; cover and freeze overnight. Use a large spoon to break mixture into a slush. Fill glasses ⅔ full; top with soda and add garnish.

Makes 8 to 10 servings

Mojito Coolers

CAROL'S TIDBITS

Rum is made from fermented sugar cane and molasses. Mild, slightly sweet light rum, also known as white or silver rum, is fermented in steel casks. Darker, more flavorful amber or gold rum is fermented in oak casks. The darkest colored, most intense flavored rum is fermented in charred oak casks.

A Mojito is a traditional Cuban highball that has become a very popular drink of choice on a hot summer day. Making the drink by the pitcher makes it very easy for entertaining.

Ingredients

⅓ cup water
⅔ cup sugar
½ cup fresh mint leaves
¼ cup fresh lime juice
2 cups light rum

2 cups club soda, chilled
Ice cubes
Mint leaves for garnish, if desired
Lime wedges for garnish, if desired

Combine water and sugar in a small saucepan. Bring mixture to a boil; stirring until sugar dissolves. Chill syrup. Combine syrup with mint leaves and lime juice in a 1½-quart pitcher; stir to crush mint leaves. Add rum and club soda. Serve over ice garnished with a fresh mint leaf and lime wedges.

Makes 4 servings

SALADS

From simple leafy mixed greens with a drizzle
of fresh dressing to citrus-infused fruit,
salads can enhance or be the best part of the meal.

Door County Mixed Greens Salad with Maple Balsamic Vinaigrette

This salad always gets rave reviews and is probably the recipe most often made by students from my cooking classes. Sweet maple and zesty balsamic are a terrific flavor combination which lends itself to a multitude of salad variations.

Ingredients

Maple Balsamic Vinaigrette

¼ cup pure maple syrup

¼ cup balsamic vinegar

1 teaspoon Dijon mustard

2 cloves garlic, minced

1 cup extra virgin olive oil

Coarse salt

Freshly ground black pepper

Salad

7 to 8 cups (5 ounces) mixed spring greens

1 to 2 apples, thinly sliced

½ cup dried tart cherries or dried sweetened cranberries

½ cup pecan halves, toasted

Crumbled blue, Roquefort, goat, or feta cheese

CAROL'S TIDBITS

Apples and cherries abound in charming Door County, Wisconsin. I love them in this salad, but wait until you try peaches, pears, and berries. And then there are walnuts, almonds, and hazelnuts. Grilled chicken is great. The salad variations are endless with this great vinaigrette!

The vinaigrette recipe makes 1½ cups; more than needed for this salad but you will want to keep it on hand. The oil solidifies in the refrigerator but quickly melts when brought to room temperature.

Combine maple syrup, vinegar, mustard, and garlic for vinaigrette in a medium mixing bowl. Slowly whisk in olive oil until well blended. Season with salt and pepper.

Toss greens in a large salad bowl with just enough dressing to lightly coat. Arrange on salad plates and garnish with apples, dried cherries, and pecans. Pass remaining dressing. Serve with crumbled cheese.

Makes 4 to 6 servings

Fruit and Greens Salad

CAROL'S TIDBITS

Toast sesame seeds on a rimmed baking sheet in a 300°F oven, stirring occasionally for 10 to 15 minutes, or toast in a skillet over low heat stirring often.

Hulled sunflower seeds may be substituted for toasted sesame seed.

One Honeycrisp or 2 Gala apples are excellent choices for this salad.

This is one of my favorite autumn and winter salads. The colors of the ingredients in this salad look like autumn leaves, and the fruits and light dressing complement many cold weather foods.

Ingredients

Salad Dressing

⅔ cup vegetable oil
¼ cup red wine or cider vinegar
3 tablespoons sugar
2 tablespoons minced fresh parsley

½ teaspoon coarse salt
Freshly ground black pepper
Dash hot pepper sauce

Salad

1 head red leaf lettuce, torn into bite-size pieces
1 head romaine lettuce, torn into bite-size pieces
4 green onions, thinly sliced
2 baby cucumbers, peeled and diced

½ cup sliced celery, if desired
Red apples, diced (do not peel)
1 can (15 ounces) Mandarin oranges, drained
¼ cup toasted sesame seeds

Combine all dressing ingredients in a 2-cup glass measure; whisk until well blended.

Combine all salad ingredients except sesame seeds in a large salad bowl. Toss with enough dressing to lightly coat. Sprinkle with sesame seeds.

Makes 8 to 10 servings

Herbed Walnut Salad

Toasted walnuts with herbs turn this simple salad into an elegant salad. A garnish of thinly sliced pears or apples adds a touch of color.

Ingredients

Walnut Vinaigrette

¼ cup vegetable oil

3 tablespoons white wine vinegar

2 tablespoons walnut or extra virgin olive oil

2 cloves garlic, minced

Coarse salt

Freshly ground black pepper

Salad

1 tablespoon walnut or extra virgin olive oil

1 cup broken walnut pieces

½ teaspoon dried basil

½ teaspoon dried rosemary

1 large head red or green leaf lettuce, torn into bite-size pieces

½ cup shaved Parmesan cheese

Sliced red pears or apples, if desired

Combine all vinaigrette ingredients in a small bowl; whisk until well blended.

Heat walnut oil in a small skillet over low heat. Add walnuts, basil, and rosemary; heat walnuts stirring frequently until walnuts are lightly toasted. Set aside to cool.

Toss lettuce with enough vinaigrette to lightly coat. Toss with half of the Parmesan and walnuts; arrange on salad plates. Garnish with remaining Parmesan, walnuts, and pear or apple slices, if desired.

Makes 6 to 8 servings

CAROL'S TIDBITS

Walnut oil intensifies the nutty flavor, but the salad is also very good with extra virgin olive oil if walnut oil is unavailable.

Substitute raspberry vinegar for white wine vinegar and garnish with fresh raspberries or blackberries.

Make extra walnuts to snack on or use for other salads.

Mixed Greens
with Maple Bacon Dressing

Can one ever get enough bacon? It is the surprise ingredient in this vinaigrette. Sweet grapes and nutty Gouda cheese are great additions to the salad.

Ingredients

Maple Bacon Dressing

1 cup vegetable or light olive oil

6 tablespoons cider vinegar

¼ cup firmly packed light brown sugar

¼ cup pure maple syrup

¼ cup chopped onion

½ teaspoon dry mustard

4 slices bacon, very crisply cooked

Salad

1 package (5 ounces) baby spinach

2 heads Bibb or 1 head Boston lettuce, torn into bite-size pieces

1 cup halved seedless red grapes

Shredded Gouda cheese

Freshly ground black pepper

Place all dressing ingredients in a food processor work bowl; process until well blended.

Toss greens in a large salad bowl with enough dressing to lightly coat. Add grapes and cheese; gently toss. Season with pepper.

Makes 6 to 8 servings

Fiddlehead Salad

This salad is named after the former Fiddlehead Restaurant & Bakery in Juneau, Alaska. Although this salad does not contain fiddlehead greens, it does remind me of spring when the young ferns peek out of the ground. Warm bacon and olive oil poured over the greens and goat cheese make a creamy dressing that looks like melting snow.

Ingredients

8 cups (5 to 6 ounces) fresh salad greens
1 tablespoon balsamic vinegar
Coarse salt
Freshly ground black pepper
½ cup (2 ounces) crumbled goat cheese

3 tablespoons extra virgin olive oil
4 slices bacon, diced
¼ cup broken walnut pieces
2 cloves garlic, minced

Toss greens in a large salad bowl with balsamic vinegar and season with salt and pepper. Crumble cheese over greens; set aside.

Heat olive oil in a medium skillet over medium-high heat. Add bacon and cook stirring often until almost crisp. Add walnuts and cook stirring often just until hot. Stir in garlic; immediately remove skillet from heat and pour drippings over greens using a slotted spoon to hold bacon and walnuts in skillet. Toss until lightly coated. Top with bacon and walnuts.

Makes 4 servings

CAROL'S TIDBITS

More robust greens like spinach, arugula, romaine, or mixed greens are perfect in this salad.

Fiddlehead greens are young, tightly coiled edible fern fronds.

Feta cheese can be used in the salad for flavor but will not melt as well as goat cheese.

To enhance the salad for a main course, add a sliced grilled chicken breast or cooked shrimp.

Baby Greens
with Chèvre Medallions

CAROL'S TIDBITS

Chèvre (SHEV-ruh or SHEV) is French for "goat."

Use dental floss to cut the cheese into clean, even slices. Slip a 10-inch length of floss under the cheese log where a slice should be cut, cross the ends, and pull tightly.

Breaded cheese medallions will be crispier if chilled on a rack before browning.

Soft and creamy goat cheese medallions with crispy crumb crusts are the star of this salad. A light lemon Dijon dressing balances the tangy cheese flavor and the raspberry garnish adds color and sweetness.

Ingredients

¼ cup olive oil
2 tablespoons freshly squeezed
   lemon juice
1 teaspoon Dijon mustard
Coarse salt
Freshly ground black pepper
⅓ cup Italian-seasoned dry
   bread crumbs
1 tablespoon grated Parmesan
   cheese

1 tablespoon sesame seeds
⅛ teaspoon garlic salt
2 logs (4 ounces each) chèvre
   goat cheese
1 egg, lightly beaten
2 tablespoons butter
1 tablespoon vegetable oil
8 cups mixed baby salad greens
   or torn leaf or Bibb lettuce
Raspberries to garnish

Combine olive oil, lemon juice, mustard, salt and pepper in a small bowl.

Combine bread crumbs, Parmesan, sesame seeds, and garlic salt on a sheet of wax paper. Cut each goat cheese log into 4 slices. Dip slices in egg and then in bread crumb mixture. Chill medallions for 2 hours.

Melt butter with vegetable oil in a medium skillet over medium-high heat. Add breaded medallions and cook until browned, about 1 to 2 minutes on each side; drain on paper towels.

Toss greens in a large salad bowl with enough dressing to lightly coat; arrange on salad plates. Top with warm medallions and raspberries.

Makes 6 to 8 servings

Greens with Roasted Beets and Goat Cheese

The sweetness of roasted beets and fresh mint are a contrast to the robust flavor of greens tossed with a Dijon vinaigrette. Add a sprinkling of goat cheese for a wonderfully delicious salad.

Ingredients

Roasted Beets
1 medium to large, or 2 small beets
1 tablespoon cider vinegar
1 tablespoon minced fresh mint
2 teaspoons sugar

2 teaspoon minced shallot
Coarse salt
Freshly ground black pepper

Vinaigrette
2 tablespoons sherry vinegar or white wine vinegar
2 teaspoons minced shallot
2 teaspoons Dijon mustard

½ teaspoon dried thyme
4 tablespoons olive or canola oil
2 tablespoons extra virgin olive oil

Salad
8 cups salad greens (mixed greens, or torn romaine, or Bibb lettuce)
Coarse salt

Freshly ground black pepper
Crumbled goat, blue, or feta cheese

Preheat oven to 400°F. Remove beet tops. Rinse beets, cut large beets in half, and wrap in foil. Roast on a second sheet of foil for 1 hour or until tender. Cool beets 15 minutes; peel and cut into julienne strips.

Combine cider vinegar, mint, sugar, shallot, salt, and pepper in a medium bowl; whisk until well blended. Add beets and toss to mix well. Set aside for 1 hour, or cover and chill overnight.

Combine sherry vinegar, shallot, mustard, and thyme in a small bowl. Combine olive oils and slowly whisk into vinegar mixture. Toss greens in a large salad bowl with enough dressing over greens to lightly coat. Season with salt and pepper. Arrange on salad plates; top with beets and sprinkle with cheese.

Makes 4 to 6 servings

Try this roasted beet salad with flavors of the Pacific Northwest. Combine ⅔ cup vegetable oil, ⅓ cup raspberry vinegar, 2 teaspoons grated orange peel, ½ teaspoon salt, and freshly ground black pepper. Toss with greens, top with diced roasted beets, sprinkle with crumbled blue cheese and toasted hazelnuts.

Beets can also be steamed for 30 to 45 minutes until tender.

Bitter frisée greens are a nice complement to the sweet beets.

St. Louis Caesar Salad

CAROL'S TIDBITS

There will be dressing and croutons to make several salads.

If desired, add a can of drained and quartered artichokes to the greens before tossing with the dressing.

Anchovy paste, a mixture of mashed anchovies, vinegar, and spices, adds zest to Caesar salads. It can be found in a tube in the canned seafood section of the grocery store.

The Hill is a historic Italian neighborhood in St. Louis.

This salad was inspired by the popular dressing served at the historic Mayfair Hotel in downtown St. Louis and salads served on The Hill.

Ingredients

Salad Dressing

1 rib celery, coarsely chopped
¼ cup chopped onion
1 clove garlic, minced
2 tablespoons fresh lemon juice
2 tablespoons Dijon mustard

1 tablespoon anchovy paste
1 teaspoon coarse black pepper
½ teaspoon sugar
2 cups mayonnaise

Croutons

2 tablespoons butter
2 tablespoons extra virgin olive oil
2 cloves garlic, slivered

4 cups French bread cubes
2 tablespoons grated Parmesan cheese

Salad

1 head romaine lettuce, torn into bite-size pieces

Shaved Parmesan cheese

Combine celery, onion, garlic, lemon juice, mustard, anchovy paste, pepper, and sugar for the dressing in a food processor work bowl; process until puréed. Add mayonnaise and process until well blended.

Preheat oven to 325°F for the croutons. Combine butter, olive oil, and garlic in a small bowl; microwave on high until butter melts, about 30 seconds. Set butter aside to infuse garlic flavor.

Spread bread cubes in a rimmed shallow baking pan. Bake 15 minutes. Strain garlic from butter and drizzle butter over bread; toss to coat. Bake until cubes are dry and lightly toasted, about 10 to 20 minutes. Sprinkle with Parmesan. Let cool before tossing in salad or storing in an airtight container.

Toss romaine in a large salad bowl with enough dressing to lightly coat. Add croutons and Parmesan. Serve immediately.

Makes 6 to 8 servings

Berry Patch
Spinach Salad

This has been a class favorite to serve for showers and luncheons, especially in the spring when strawberries are at their luscious best.

Ingredients

⅓ to ½ cup sugar

4 tablespoons raspberry or cider vinegar

1 teaspoon poppy seeds

½ teaspoon seasoned salt

4 tablespoons olive oil

1 package (10 ounces) baby spinach

1 pound fresh strawberries, hulled and quartered

1 avocado, halved, pitted, peeled, and cubed

1 cup pecan halves, toasted

Combine sugar, vinegar, poppy seed, and seasoned salt in a small bowl. Slowly whisk in oil until well blended.

Toss spinach in a large salad bowl with enough dressing to lightly coat. Add strawberries, avocado, and pecans; gently toss.

Makes 6 to 8 servings

CAROL'S TIDBITS

Original recipe used ½ cup sugar when the class fell in love with the salad. I use ⅓ cup when I make it and often replace part of the sugar with artificial sweetener.

To help dissolve the sugar, microwave sugar and vinegar on high for 10 to 15 seconds.

I use Lawry's seasoned salt.

Fiesta
Corn Salad

CAROL'S TIDBITS

Grilling, or quickly cooking corn on the cob in boiling water for 3 minutes, brings out sweetness in the corn. Peppers and onions may also be grilled for enhanced flavor.

I still follow the rule of eating corn on the cob only in the summer when it is at its peak locally. When I was growing up, the pot of water was boiling when we went to the garden and picked corn for dinner. The sweet, tender kernels almost exploded in my mouth and that continues to be my expectation.

One bag (16 ounces) frozen corn kernels, thawed and drained, may be substituted in the winter.

When fresh corn is at its peak, this salad is a great accompaniment to grilled pork chops and burgers. It can be served as a salad or a salsa with the meat.

Ingredients

6 ears corn
1 red or ½ red and ½ green bell
  pepper, diced
¼ cup chopped green or red onion
¼ cup sliced ripe olives
2 tablespoons chopped Italian parsley
3 tablespoons olive oil

2 tablespoons fresh lemon juice
1 tablespoon red wine vinegar
1 clove garlic, minced
½ teaspoon coarse salt
½ teaspoon ground cumin
½ teaspoon chili powder
⅛ teaspoon cayenne pepper

Preheat grill to medium-high. Place corn on grid; grill turning occasionally until beginning to char, about 8 minutes. Cool corn; cut kernels from cob with serrated knife.

Combine corn with bell pepper, onion, olives, and parsley in a large bowl. Combine olive oil, lemon juice, wine vinegar, garlic, salt, cumin, chili powder, and cayenne pepper in a small bowl; add to corn mixture and toss until lightly coated. Cover and chill at least 2 hours before serving.

Makes 6 to 8 servings

Napa Cabbage Coleslaw

Napa cabbage is often used in stir-fry foods, but is especially refreshing tossed with the light Asian dressing in this coleslaw.

Ingredients

Asian Dressing
¼ cup vegetable oil

2 tablespoons sugar

2 tablespoons rice or white wine vinegar

1 tablespoon chopped fresh parsley

1 teaspoon soy sauce

½ teaspoon grated fresh ginger

¼ teaspoon coarse salt

Dash hot pepper sauce

Coleslaw
1 medium head napa cabbage, thinly sliced (4 to 5 cups)

1 cup shredded carrots (2 large)

1 can (8 ounces) sliced water chestnuts, drained and rinsed

¼ cup sliced green onion

½ cup slivered almonds, toasted

2 tablespoons sesame seeds, toasted

Combine all dressing ingredients in a small container with tight-fitting lid; cover and shake to blend well. Refrigerate at least 2 hours to blend flavors.

Toss cabbage, carrots, water chestnuts, and onion in a large salad bowl with enough dressing to lightly coat. Add almonds and sesame seeds just before serving; toss gently.

Makes 8 to 10 servings

Cabbage Patch Salad

CAROL'S TIDBITS

The peanut topping should be crunchy when served. Keep it in a small plastic bag to add at the last minute.

You will be asked to share this recipe when you take it to the next potluck picnic. The peanut and Parmesan topping is the secret to its popularity.

Ingredients

4 to 6 cups shredded cabbage
2 cups bite-size cauliflower florets
1 cup bite-size broccoli florets
½ cup sliced radishes
¼ cup chopped onion
1 cup mayonnaise
5 tablespoons grated Parmesan
   cheese, divided

2 tablespoons granulated sugar
¼ teaspoon coarse salt
Freshly ground black pepper
1 tablespoon butter
½ cup chopped peanuts

Combine cabbage, cauliflower, broccoli, radishes, and onion in a large salad bowl. Combine mayonnaise, 3 tablespoons of the Parmesan, sugar, salt and pepper in a small bowl. Add dressing to vegetables; gently toss.

Melt butter in a small skillet over medium heat; add peanuts and cook until golden. Remove from heat and stir in remaining 2 tablespoons Parmesan. Sprinkle over salad just before serving.

Makes 8 to 10 servings

Cold Cauliflower Nivernais

This is an iconic salad made popular by a small inn in Stony Brook, New York. The classic way to serve it is in lettuce cups. A more trendy way is to serve it on thin wedges of iceberg lettuce topped with crispy bacon and blue cheese.

Ingredients

4 cups bite-size cauliflower florets
⅔ cup mayonnaise
3 tablespoons dairy sour cream
2 tablespoons Dijon mustard
1 tablespoon heavy whipping cream
1 teaspoon lemon juice

Coarse salt
Freshly ground black pepper
Bibb lettuce cups or thin wedges iceberg lettuce
Diced pimiento or red bell pepper
Chopped fresh parsley

Cook cauliflower in 1-inch salted water in a large covered saucepan over high heat just until crisp-tender; drain and rinse under cold water to rapidly chill. Drain well and chill.

Combine mayonnaise, sour cream, mustard, cream, and lemon juice in a small bowl; cover and chill.

Just before serving, toss cauliflower with dressing in a large bowl; season with salt and pepper. Serve in Bibb lettuce cups or on a thin wedge of iceberg lettuce. Garnish with pimiento or red bell pepper and chopped parsley.

Makes 6 to 8 servings

CAROL'S TIDBITS

Skip the lettuce and serve the cauliflower mixture as a side salad. Substitute broccoli for all or part of the cauliflower.

Charlie's
Potato Salad

CAROL'S TIDBITS

Charlie's made their own mayonnaise, but prepared regular or reduced-fat mayonnaise is an excellent shortcut.

To hard cook eggs without grey rings, place eggs in a small saucepan and cover with cold water; cook over high heat until boiling. Cover, remove from heat and let stand 10 minutes. Cool immediately with cold water and peel.

Charlie's Café Exceptional was a Minneapolis fine dining icon for nearly fifty years. Most remembered about the restaurant was the potato salad served to all guests as an appetizer. This creamy potato salad has a wonderful balance of flavors with few ingredients.

Ingredients

2½ pounds red potatoes, cooked, peeled and cubed (5 cups cubed)
¼ cup diced celery
2 tablespoons chopped green onion
2 tablespoons diced red bell pepper

3 hard-cooked eggs, diced or sliced
1¼ cups mayonnaise
1 teaspoon coarse salt
¼ teaspoon ground white pepper

Combine potatoes, celery, onion, red pepper, and eggs in a large mixing bowl. Combine mayonnaise, salt, and pepper in a small bowl. Add to potatoes and gently toss. Chill at least 2 hours before serving for flavors to blend.

Makes 8 to 10 servings

Charlie's Mayonnaise

1 pasteurized egg yolk
1 teaspoon sugar
1 teaspoon dry mustard
¼ teaspoon salt
⅛ teaspoon cayenne pepper
1 tablespoon lemon juice or white vinegar
1 cup vegetable oil

Combine mayonnaise ingredients except oil in a blender container; blend on medium speed while slowly adding oil. Blend until thickened. Add additional lemon juice or vinegar for a more tangy flavor.

Roasted Potato Salad

This potato salad is especially good served slightly warm. I like to serve it with bratwurst or grilled salmon.

Ingredients

2½ to 3 pounds red potatoes
¼ cup olive oil
Coarse salt
Freshly ground black pepper
½ cup mayonnaise

½ cup dairy sour cream
1 tablespoon chopped fresh dill
1 tablespoon prepared horseradish
1 tablespoon milk
1 teaspoon Dijon mustard

Preheat oven to 425°F. Scrub potatoes and cut into 1-inch cubes. Toss potatoes with olive oil and spread on a rimmed baking sheet; season with salt and pepper. Cover with foil and bake 15 minutes. Uncover and turn potatoes with spatula. Continue to roast, stirring once, for 15 to 20 additional minutes or until tender and golden brown.

Combine mayonnaise, sour cream, dill, horseradish, and mustard; pour over potatoes and toss until coated. Season with salt and pepper.

Makes 8 to 10 servings

CAROL'S TIDBITS

Potatoes can also be cooked on a tray on the grill until tender and golden brown. Cooking time will be slightly shorter. Flavor will be wonderful!

If the warm potatoes absorb too much dressing, just add a bit more mayo and sour cream.

Look for prepared horseradish in the dairy department. Store the jar upside down in the refrigerator to preserve its flavor and creamy color.

Cranberry
Wine Salad

Sometimes it is hard to beat a gelatin salad and this is the perfect one to serve with Thanksgiving dinner.

Ingredients

2 cups boiling water
1 package (6 ounces) cranberry gelatin
½ cup sugar
Dash salt
2 cans (8 ounces each) crushed
   pineapple in juice, undrained

2 cups (7 ounces) fresh cranberries,
   chopped
¾ cup ruby port wine
1 cup chopped pecans or walnuts,
   if desired

Cream Cheese Topping
1 package (8 ounces) cream cheese,
   softened

1 cup (8 ounces) dairy sour cream
1 teaspoon grated orange peel

Dissolve gelatin, sugar, and salt in boiling water in a large mixing bowl. Stir in pineapple, cranberries, and port wine. Chill until gelatin mixture begins to set up. Stir in chopped nuts and pour into an 8-cup mold; chill until firm.

Combine cream cheese, sour cream, and orange peel in a medium bowl; stir until well blended.

Unmold salad onto a platter and serve with Cream Cheese Topping.

Makes 12 servings

Minted Melon Compote

Melon chilled in a minty, citrus-flavored syrup is especially refreshing on a warm summer day. For frosty cold fruit, chill the fruit in the freezer for an hour before serving. Garnish with fresh mint and orange peel.

Ingredients

½ cup water
6 tablespoons sugar
2 tablespoons chopped fresh mint
2 tablespoons orange juice
1 tablespoon fresh lemon juice

1 honeydew melon
1 cantaloupe melon
Chopped fresh mint, if desired
Grated orange peel, if desired

Combine water and sugar in a 2-cup glass measure; microwave on high for 2 minutes stirring once. Stir in mint, orange juice, and lemon juice. Chill mixture for 1 hour.

Cut melons into balls or cubes and place in a serving dish. Strain mint syrup over fruit; toss fruit until well mixed. Cover and chill until serving time. Garnish with chopped mint and orange peel. Serve with a slotted spoon or in individual dishes.

Makes about 6 cups fruit

CAROL'S TIDBITS

Make a larger quantity of the mint syrup and store in the refrigerator for up to 2 weeks to have available to drizzle over most any fruit. I especially like the syrup on melons, watermelon, and berries.

The syrup also makes delicious mint sweet tea.

Layered Fruit Salad with Honey-Lime Dressing

CAROL'S TIDBITS

Layer fruit in tall glasses for individual servings.

Crystallized or candied ginger is fresh ginger that has been cooked in syrup, coated with coarse sugar and dried; store in an air-tight container. Look for it in the produce section with the dried mushrooms and peppers or in the spice section of the baking aisle.

Crystallized ginger is good on fruit and ice cream, or in baked goods and tea.

Layer fresh fruits of the season in a clear bowl or toss with dressing in a hollowed-out watermelon for a festive occasion. There are many red, white, and blue fruit possibilities for a patriotic theme. The Honey-Lime Dressing complements most any fruit.

Ingredients

Honey-Lime Dressing

⅓ cup honey

¼ cup orange juice

2 teaspoons grated lime peel

¼ cup fresh lime juice

2 tablespoons finely chopped crystallized ginger

6 to 8 cups fresh fruit

Combine honey, orange juice, lime peel and juice, and crystallized ginger in a small container with a tight-fitting lid; cover and shake until honey is dissolved.

Layer or combine choice of fruits in a serving bowl. Drizzle dressing over fruit. Refrigerate for 1 to 2 hours before serving.

Makes 6 to 8 servings

Fruit Choices

Red Fruits: Watermelon, strawberries, raspberries, cherries, plums, red grapes
Blue Fruits: Blueberries, blackberries, grapes
Light-Colored Fruits: Honeydew melon, pineapple, bananas, pears, apples
Yellow/Orange Fruits: Cantaloupe, peaches, nectarines, apricots, oranges, pineapple, papaya, mangos
Green Fruits: Honeydew melon, kiwi, green grapes

SOUPS

Nothing beats a cup of rich, creamy soup or a
steaming bowl of hearty soup loaded with fresh
vegetables and flavorful meats.
This is comfort food at its best.

Tuscan Vegetable Soup

The Tuscany region of Italy is known for its classic vegetable and bean soups. You will love the addition of fresh spinach just before serving.

Ingredients

1 tablespoon olive oil
1 cup sliced carrots
½ cup chopped onion
½ cup sliced celery
2 cloves garlic, minced
½ teaspoon coarse salt
3 cans (14.5 ounces each) reduced sodium chicken broth
2 cans (14.5 ounces each) cannellini beans, drained and lightly rinsed
1 can (14.5 ounces) tomatoes with basil, garlic, and oregano

1 cup diced zucchini
½ cup diced red bell pepper
1 teaspoon dried basil
½ teaspoon dried oregano
¼ teaspoon dried thyme leaves
2 cups packed (2 ounces) coarsely chopped fresh spinach
Coarse salt
Freshly ground black pepper
Freshly grated Parmesan cheese

Heat olive oil in a Dutch oven over medium-high heat. Add carrots, onion, celery, garlic, and salt; cook stirring often until beginning to get tender. Stir in broth; bring to a boil. Stir in beans, tomatoes, zucchini, bell pepper, basil, oregano, and thyme; return to a boil. Reduce heat and simmer for 15 minutes. Stir in spinach and cook just until spinach wilts. Season with salt and pepper. Serve with Parmesan cheese.

Makes 8 cups soup

CAROL'S TIDBITS

Rinsing beans reduces sodium, but flavor will be lost if rinsed too thoroughly.

Serve with crostini (page 17); ladle soup over them or serve on the side.

For extra flavor, add the Parmesan cheese rind to the soup while it is cooking.

Hearty Italian Sausage Soup

Italian sausage and cheese tortellini add heartiness to this Italian vegetable soup, making it very satisfying on a cold winter day. Serve with crusty bread and your meal is complete.

Ingredients

1 pound bulk Italian sausage
2 cups cubed zucchini
1½ cups sliced carrots
1 cup chopped onion
1 green bell pepper, diced
2 cloves garlic, minced
1 can (28 ounces) crushed tomatoes in tomato puree
2 cans (14.5 ounces each) reduced sodium beef broth
1 can (14.5 ounces) reduced sodium chicken broth

1 cup water
½ cup dry red or white wine
1 tablespoon chopped fresh or 1 teaspoon dried basil
1½ teaspoons chopped fresh or ½ teaspoon dried oregano
½ teaspoon freshly ground black pepper
1 package (9 ounces) refrigerated cheese tortellini
Coarse salt
Freshly grated Parmesan cheese

Cook sausage in a Dutch oven over medium-high heat stirring often until browned. Blot sausage with a paper towel to remove any excess fat. Stir in zucchini, carrots, onion, bell pepper, and garlic; cook stirring often until vegetables begin to soften. Stir in tomatoes, broths, water, wine, and seasonings; bring to a boil.

Stir in pasta and cook until pasta is just tender. Season with salt and additional herbs, if desired. Serve with grated Parmesan cheese.

Makes 12 cups soup

Baked Potato Soup

There is something about baked potato soup on a cold winter night that just hits the spot. It is warm and creamy, but it might be the crisp bacon and cheese toppings that are so comforting.

Ingredients

4 baking potatoes (8 to 9 ounces each)
4 tablespoons butter
½ cup chopped onion
⅓ cup flour
2 teaspoons coarse salt
4 cups (1 quart) milk
2 cups or 1 can (14.5 ounces) reduced sodium chicken broth

1 cup (8 ounces) dairy sour cream
Freshly ground black pepper
Shredded Cheddar cheese
Crumbled cooked bacon
Sliced green onion or chopped chives

Preheat oven to 400°F. Scrub potatoes and pierce several times with fork or knife tip. Place potatoes on oven rack and bake 1 hour or until tender. Cool enough to cut potatoes in half lengthwise and scoop pulp out of the shell. Coarsely mash pulp with a fork; set aside. If desired, skins can be used to make baked potato skins.

Melt butter in a Dutch oven over medium heat; add onion and cook stirring often just until tender. Stir in flour and salt; cook until bubbly. Stir in milk and broth; cook until mixture bubbles and thickens. Stir in half of the potatoes and blend with an immersion blender or portable mixer. Stir in remaining potatoes and sour cream; cook until heated. Season with salt and pepper to taste. Serve soup topped with cheese, bacon, and green onions or chives.

Makes 10 cups soup

Baked Potato Skins: Brush the baked potato skins with melted butter, sprinkle with shredded Cheddar cheese, and bake at 400°F until cheese is melted, about 10 minutes. Serve with your favorite baked potato toppings.

CAROL'S TIDBITS

Potatoes have best flavor when baked in a conventional oven, but can be baked in the microwave for faster cooking time.

What is a baking potato? Baking potatoes have thick, light-colored skins and a dry, mealy texture when baked. Potatoes with red skins have a waxy, gummy texture when baked. Potatoes with yellow skins, such as Yukon golds, have a texture in between, are very flavorful, and can be used in this soup.

Maple Butternut Squash Bisque

Butternut squash is sweet and nutty with a creamy-textured flesh. Pick squash that are heavy for their size; look for squash with large necks as this is where most of the pulp will be found. The seed cavity is in the bulb end.

Microwave any squash on high for 2 minutes to make it easy and safer to cut through the hard shell and remove seeds.

Use pure maple syrup, not sweet maple-flavored pancake syrup.

Students in my classes <u>loved</u> this soup! I like to serve it as a first course or with a salad. Be sure to add the drizzle of maple syrup for the crowning touch.

Ingredients

3 to 3½ pounds butternut squash
6 tablespoons butter
1 cup chopped onion
¼ cup flour
1 can (14.5 ounces) reduced sodium chicken or vegetable broth

1½ cups milk
¾ cup half-and-half
¼ cup pure maple syrup
1 teaspoon coarse salt
Dash cayenne pepper
Maple syrup for garnish

Preheat oven to 375°F. Line a 2-inch deep baking dish with foil; set aside.

Microwave each whole squash on high for 2 minutes. Cut squash in half and remove seeds with a spoon. Place squash, cut-side down, in prepared baking dish. Pour enough hot water into dish to cover about 1 inch of the squash. Bake until squash can be easily pierced with a knife, about 1 hour. Let squash cool for 30 minutes or until cool enough to handle. Scoop squash from shells.

Melt butter in a Dutch oven over medium heat. Add onion and cook stirring occasionally until lightly browned, about 10 to 15 minutes. Add flour; stirring constantly and cook about 2 minutes. Stir in cooked squash, broth, milk, half-and-half, maple syrup, salt, and cayenne. Bring soup to a boil over high heat; reduce heat and simmer, stirring often until squash is very soft and soup is thickened, about 15 to 20 minutes.

Remove soup from heat. Purée soup using either an immersion blender or food processor. If using a food processor, purée soup in small batches. If soup is too thick, add additional milk or broth. Season soup with salt and pepper to taste.

Ladle soup into serving bowls. Drizzle with maple syrup or pass a pitcher of maple syrup at the table.

Makes 9 cups

Creamy Tomato Bisque

Tomato soup rises to a new level with this quick and easy bisque that is delicious any time of the year. The basil garnish adds a touch of freshness.

Ingredients

2 tablespoons butter
1 cup chopped onion
2 cloves garlic, minced
2 tablespoons flour
1 can (14.5 ounces) reduced sodium chicken broth
1 can (28 ounces) diced tomatoes with juice

1 bay leaf
1 tablespoon brown sugar
1 teaspoon dried basil
¼ teaspoon coarse salt
Freshly ground black pepper
2 cups half-and-half
Thin strips of fresh basil

Melt butter in a large saucepan over low heat. Add onion and garlic; cook stirring often until onion is very tender. Stir in flour and cook until bubbly. Stir in broth, tomatoes, bay leaf, brown sugar, basil, salt, and pepper. Simmer uncovered for 15 minutes.

Strain solids from liquid; set liquid aside. Place solids in a blender or food processor work bowl; process until puréed. With machine running, pour reserved liquid through feed tube and process until smooth.

Pour half-and-half into the saucepan and slowly add the tomato purée. Heat over medium heat just until hot but not boiling. Season with additional salt, pepper, and brown sugar. Garnish with fresh basil.

Makes 6 cups

CAROL'S TIDBITS

Always add acid ingredients, such as tomatoes, slowly to dairy products to prevent curdling. Do not boil the combined mixture.

The culinary term for thin strips or shreds of basil is a basil chiffonade. The literal translation for this term is "made of rags."

This soup is extra delicious served with croutons. See page 50 for recipe.

Chicken Stock

Necks, backs, wings, legs, and thighs are good pieces of chicken to use when making stock. Add a chicken breast or two during last 30 minutes of cooking if wanting to use meat in a recipe.

One 5-pound chicken = 3 cups diced meat. One whole bone-in chicken breast = 1 to 1¼ cups diced meat.

Leftover turkey carcass may be substituted for the roasting chicken or pieces.

If flavor of stock is weak, enhance flavor with bouillon cubes adding one cube at a time.

Nothing is better than homemade stock for chicken soup. It is easy to make and portions can be frozen for future soups and entrées.

Ingredients

5-pound roasting chicken or combination of chicken pieces with bones
4 quarts water
1 large onion, sliced
3 carrots, sliced
3 ribs celery, sliced

½ cup parsley sprigs including stems
1½ teaspoons coarse salt
½ teaspoon dried thyme
10 whole peppercorns
1 bay leaf

Combine chicken and water in a large, deep, narrow stockpot. Slowly bring to a boil. Reduce heat and simmer uncovered for 30 minutes. Skim off any foam that may appear. Add remaining ingredients; simmer uncovered (or loosely covered if pot is more wide than deep) for 2 hours.

Strain broth, pressing on chicken and vegetables with back of spoon to extract as much broth and flavor as possible. Remove meat from bones; discard bones and vegetables. Refrigerate broth as soon as it is no longer steaming. Use meat in Chunky Chicken Noodle Soup (on following page) or other recipes. Broth may be refrigerated for up to 3 days or frozen up to 6 months. Remove fat from chilled broth before using.

Makes 12 cups broth

Note: For a dark stock, especially good in pork and veal dishes, roast chicken and vegetables in a roasting pan at 300˚F for 30 to 40 minutes until browned. Transfer chicken and vegetables to a stockpot. Deglaze the roasting pan with 2 cups of the stock cooking water. Add 1 tablespoon tomato paste to the stockpot along with remaining 14 cups water; continue as directed in recipe above.

Chunky Chicken
Noodle Soup

Not only is chicken noodle soup one of the best remedies for a cold, it is nearly everyone's favorite soup. This good old-fashioned soup will always be a winner!

Ingredients

8 cups (64 ounces) chicken stock
1 cup chopped onion
2 medium carrots, sliced (1 to 1½ cups)
1 rib celery, sliced (½ to 1 cup)
¾ teaspoon coarse salt
3 cups diced cooked chicken
2 cups short noodles

2 tablespoons chopped fresh parsley
Coarse salt
Freshly ground black pepper
2 to 3 tablespoons dry white wine or vermouth, or a few drops vinegar or lemon juice

Heat broth in a Dutch oven over high heat just until boiling. Add onion, carrots, celery, and the ¾ teaspoon salt; return to a boil. Reduce heat; cover and simmer for 10 minutes. Stir in chicken, noodles, and parsley; cook loosely covered until noodles are tender. Season with salt and pepper. Add wine to boost overall flavor.

Makes 8 cups soup

CAROL'S TIDBITS

Use recipe on page 68 to make homemade chicken stock.

If making ahead or storing leftovers, strain soup and store broth separate from noodles, vegetables, and chicken.

A rotisserie chicken is a good source for cooked chicken. Expect to get 3 cups diced meat from one chicken.

The addition of wine or vinegar brings the flavor alive.

Soupe à la Oignon (French Onion Soup)

CAROL'S TIDBITS

The French began putting bread slices in their onion soup to make it a complete meal. It makes the soup so tasty, it is now an expected feature of French onion soup.

Yellow onions are full-flavored and turn a rich, dark brown when cooked. They give French onion soup its tangy, sweet flavor.

Mild white onions have a sweet flavor when cooked and are often used in salads and Mexican cuisine.

There are many reasons to go to France, but French onion soup does not need to be one of them. Make this soup and enjoy it with a glass of wine. You may think you are in Paris . . . momentarily.

Ingredients

4 tablespoons butter
2 tablespoons vegetable oil
2 pounds yellow onions, sliced
1 teaspoon coarse salt
½ teaspoon sugar
½ teaspoon freshly ground black pepper
3 tablespoons flour
2 quarts (64 ounces) beef stock
⅔ cup dry white wine

3 to 4 tablespoons Cognac, if desired
12 to 16 slices French bread baguette, about ½ inch thick
Extra virgin olive oil
1 large clove garlic, cut in half
2 cups shredded Gruyère cheese (8 ounces)
Grated Parmesan

Melt butter with oil in a large, heavy saucepan over medium heat. Stir in onions; cover and cook over low heat for 15 minutes. Stir in salt, sugar, and pepper; cook uncovered, stirring occasionally for 20 to 30 minutes until onions are golden brown.

Stir in flour and cook 2 to 3 minutes. Stir in beef stock, wine, and Cognac; cover and simmer for 30 to 40 minutes.

Preheat oven to 400°F. Place baguette slices on a parchment-lined baking sheet. Bake 5 minutes. Lightly brush with olive oil. Turn slices over, brush with olive oil, and bake 5 additional minutes or until golden brown. Rub each slice with cut garlic.

Preheat broiler. Ladle soup into oven-proof soup bowls. Top with baguette slices and sprinkle with Gruyère and Parmesan. Broil until cheese is bubbly and lightly browned.

Makes 6 to 8 servings

Broccoli
Cheese Soup

There is not a lot new to say about broccoli cheese soup. It is just a classic family favorite not to be forgotten when looking for a quick and tasty supper idea. The new twist is to make it with cauliflower or a combination of broccoli and cauliflower.

Ingredients

4 tablespoons butter
½ cup coarsely shredded carrot
¼ cup chopped onion
1 clove garlic, minced
4 tablespoons flour
1 can (14.5 ounces) reduced sodium chicken broth
2 cups (16 ounces) milk

1 teaspoon dry mustard
¼ teaspoon ground white pepper
3 cups finely chopped broccoli or cauliflower
8 ounces (2 cups) shredded sharp Cheddar cheese
¼ teaspoon hot pepper sauce
Coarse salt

CAROL'S TIDBITS

Another new twist is to use fontina cheese or a combination of fontina and Cheddar.

I prefer fresh broccoli or cauliflower, but frozen can be used.

Melt butter in a large saucepan over medium-high heat. Add carrot, onion, and garlic; cook stirring often until onion is tender. Stir in flour and cook until bubbly. Stir in broth, milk, mustard, and pepper; cook until beginning to thicken.

Stir in broccoli; cook over medium-low heat stirring occasionally for 15 minutes. Gradually stir in cheese; continue stirring until cheese is melted. Stir in hot sauce and season with salt.

Makes 6 cups

Bistro
Seafood Chowder

CAROL'S TIDBITS

Bay scallops are small and sea scallops are large. I correlate the size of the scallops to the size of the water body they come from (small bay, large sea).

Garnish the chowder with extra whole cooked shrimp and fresh basil.

If you are a clam chowder fan, you will love this more sophisticated rich, thick, and chunky soup loaded with shrimp, scallops, and crab.

Ingredients

8 tablespoons (1 stick) butter, divided
1 large potato, diced (1½ to 2 cups)
2 medium carrots, chopped (1 cup)
2 ribs celery, chopped (1 cup)
12 ounces large shrimp, peeled, deveined, and diced (2 cups)
8 ounces bay or cut-up sea scallops (1 cup)
1 can (6.5 ounces) crabmeat (1 cup)
6 (48 ounces) cups milk

1 cup (8 ounces) heavy whipping cream
1 cup (8 ounces) reduced sodium chicken broth
1 teaspoon coarse salt
½ cup flour
1 teaspoon dried, or 1 tablespoon minced fresh basil
½ teaspoon freshly ground black pepper

Melt 2 tablespoons of the butter in a Dutch oven over medium-high heat. Add potato, carrots, and celery; cook stirring often until vegetables are tender. Add shrimp, scallops, and crabmeat with their juices, milk, cream, broth, and salt; cook stirring occasionally just to the boiling point.

Meanwhile, melt remaining 6 tablespoons butter in a small saucepan over medium heat. Stir in flour and cook stirring constantly until mixture is very bubbly. Add basil and pepper. Stir mixture into soup and cook over medium heat stirring often until soup thickens. Season with salt and pepper to taste. Remove from heat and let stand for 5 minutes before serving.

Makes 12 cups

Minnesota Wild Rice Soup

Minnesota is the land of lakes and wild rice. A colorful mix of diced vegetables makes this wild rice soup both eye-pleasing and extra flavorful. It is perfect for autumn and holiday entertaining.

Ingredients

8 ounces bacon, diced
1 red bell pepper, diced
1 yellow bell pepper, diced
1 green bell pepper, diced
2 cups chopped onion
1½ cups diced carrots
1 cup diced celery
2 cloves garlic, minced
1 bay leaf
2 teaspoons dried basil
1 teaspoon dried thyme

1 teaspoon coarse salt
8 cups (64 ounces) reduced sodium
  chicken broth or stock
8 ounces wild rice
½ cup (1 stick) butter
½ cup flour
2 cups (16 ounces) half-and-half
1 tablespoon Worcestershire sauce
¼ to ½ teaspoon hot pepper sauce
Coarse salt
Freshly ground black pepper

Cook bacon in a Dutch oven over medium heat stirring often until crisp; remove drippings. Add peppers, onion, carrots, celery, garlic, bay leaf, basil, thyme, and salt; cover and cook over medium heat for 5 minutes. Add broth and bring to a boil. Add wild rice; reduce heat, cover, simmer for 1 hour or until rice is tender.

Melt butter in a medium saucepan over medium heat. Stir in flour and cook stirring constantly until bubbly and lightly browned. Stir in half-and-half and cook stirring often until thickened. Add to soup along with Worcestershire and hot pepper sauce. Simmer for 15 minutes. Season with salt and pepper.

Makes 12 cups

Turkey
Wild Rice Soup

CAROL'S TIDBITS

Turkey may be omitted or substituted with chicken, ham, or a combination of meats.

Wild rice gets softer and absorbs more liquid as it cooks and also when leftovers are refrigerated or frozen.

Cultivated wild rice tends to be darker colored, firmer and slower to absorb liquid than wild rice grown on cold Minnesota lakes and harvested in the traditional Native American way.

This very popular version of Minnesota's state soup is a wonderful way to use leftover Thanksgiving turkey, but this is not a once-a-year only soup at our house. Oven-roasted turkey from the deli is a great alternative for those other times.

Ingredients

5 cups (40 ounces) chicken stock or reduced sodium broth

1 package (4 ounces) wild rice, about ⅔ cup

½ cup sliced green onions

6 tablespoons butter

⅓ cup flour

½ teaspoon coarse salt

¼ teaspoon poultry seasoning

⅛ teaspoon ground black pepper

2 cups half-and-half

1½ to 2 cups cubed cooked turkey

8 slices bacon, diced and cooked crisp

3 tablespoons dry sherry

Salt and pepper to taste

Pimiento and chopped fresh parsley for garnish

Dry sherry

Combine chicken stock, wild rice, and green onion in a Dutch oven and bring to a boil over medium-high heat. Reduce heat, cover, and simmer for 45 to 60 minutes or until rice is tender.

Melt butter in a medium saucepan over medium-high heat. Stir in flour, salt, poultry seasoning, and pepper; cook stirring often until bubbly and smooth. Stir in half-and-half and cook stirring constantly until mixture thickens, about 5 minutes.

Stir creamed mixture into soup; add turkey, bacon, and sherry; simmer over low heat for 15 minutes. Season with salt and pepper. Garnish with pimiento and parsley. Drizzle additional sherry over soup when served.

Makes 9 cups soup

White Lightening Chili

White beans, chicken, and corn may be a different twist to traditional chili, but every bit as delicious. This is a great game-day comfort and party food.

Ingredients

1 tablespoon vegetable oil
½ cup chopped onion
2 cloves garlic, minced
2 cans (16 ounces each) Great Northern beans, drained and lightly rinsed
2 cups shredded cooked chicken or turkey
2 cups frozen white or yellow corn kernels
1 can (14.5 ounces) reduced sodium chicken broth

1 can (4.5 ounces) chopped green chiles
1 to 1½ teaspoons ground cumin
1 teaspoon chili powder
¾ teaspoon dried oregano leaves
½ teaspoon coarse salt
⅛ teaspoon cayenne pepper
Dairy sour cream
Shredded Monterey Jack cheese
Tortilla chips

Heat oil in a large saucepan over medium-high heat. Add onion and garlic; cook stirring often until tender. Stir in beans, chicken, corn, broth, chiles, 1 teaspoon cumin, chili powder, oregano, salt, and cayenne pepper; bring to a boil. Reduce heat and cover; simmer for 20 to 30 minutes.

Stir in ½ teaspoon additional cumin if a more spicy chili is preferred. Serve with sour cream, Monterey Jack cheese, and tortilla chips.

Makes 8 cups chili

CAROL'S TIDBITS

Set out bowls of the garnishes and let everyone dress their own chili. Other tasty garnishes are diced tomatoes, sliced green onions, and chopped cilantro.

Chili thickens as it cooks and stands. Add additional broth if a thinner consistency is desired.

For a vegetarian chili, omit chicken and use vegetable broth.

Easiest Ever
Chili

CAROL'S TIDBITS

Chili requires Cheddar cheese served on the side!

I use a mixture of flavorful ground chuck and more lean sirloin, or an 85% to 90% lean ground beef.

This is a longtime staple at our house and so easy that it was one of the first recipes our sons mastered when they began cooking. This kid-friendly chili can become more complex through the addition of hot chili beans, onions, garlic, and higher levels of seasonings.

Ingredients

1½ pounds lean ground beef
1 tablespoon chili powder
1½ teaspoons ground cumin

½ teaspoon Lawry's seasoned salt
1 can (15.5 ounces) mild chili beans
1 can (11.5 ounces) tomato juice

Crumble ground beef into a microwave-safe casserole dish; microwave on high for 5 minutes. Drain excess fat and break up meat with a spoon. Sprinkle meat with seasonings and microwave for 2 additional minutes. Stir in beans and tomato juice.

Cover casserole and microwave for 5 minutes; stir. Taste and adjust seasonings, if desired. Cover and cook for 5 additional minutes.

Makes 6 servings

BREADS

What can be better than the aroma
of bread baking? Enjoying these breads fresh from
the oven. It will be difficult to choose
which one to make first.

Cranberry Scones

If you are an overnight guest at our home, you are very likely to have these scones for breakfast. Be sure to serve the Orange Honey Butter with them!

Ingredients

1½ cups flour
¼ cup sugar
1½ teaspoons baking powder
¼ teaspoon baking soda
¼ teaspoon salt
⅛ teaspoon ground cinnamon
Dash ground allspice

¾ teaspoon grated orange peel
5 tablespoons cold butter, cubed
½ cup buttermilk
½ cup fresh cranberries
¼ cup coarsely chopped pecans
1 tablespoon butter
Coarse or granulated sugar

Orange Honey Butter
½ cup (1 stick) butter, softened
1 tablespoon honey

1 teaspoon grated orange peel

Preheat oven to 400°F. Line a baking sheet with parchment paper. Combine flour, sugar, baking powder, baking soda, salt, cinnamon, and allspice in a large mixing bowl. Cut cubed butter into flour until the mixture is consistency of coarse crumbs. Stir in buttermilk just until flour is moistened. For a sweeter cranberry flavor, chop cranberries just until most berries are cut in half. Stir cranberries and pecans into dough.

Form dough into a ball on a lightly floured surface. Pat dough into a ¾-inch-thick circle; cut into 8 wedges. Place wedges on the prepared baking sheet; brush with melted butter and sprinkle with sugar. Bake 12 to 15 minutes or until lightly browned.

Combine butter, honey, and orange peel in a small mixer bowl; beat until fluffy. Serve with warm scones.

Makes 8 scones

CAROL'S TIDBITS

I like to make mini scones when there are other food options. For mini scones, flatten dough into a square about ½-inch thick. Cut into 12 to 16 squares. Bake 10 to 12 minutes or until lightly browned.

Chop cranberries just before adding into dough to minimize bleeding. ⅓ cup sweetened dried cranberries may be substituted for fresh cranberries.

Fresh blueberries may be substituted for cranberries. Do not chop blueberries.

Spicy Cranberry Muffins with Orange Honey Butter

These muffins were a hit in my first Country Inn Christmas class. A blend of sweet spices and orange peel complement tart cranberries in these delicious muffins.

Ingredients

2 cups flour
1 cup sugar
1½ teaspoons baking powder
1½ teaspoons ground nutmeg
1 teaspoon ground cinnamon
½ teaspoon baking soda
½ teaspoon ground ginger

½ cup solid vegetable shortening
2 eggs, slightly beaten
2 teaspoons grated orange peel
¾ cup orange juice
1 tablespoon vanilla extract
1½ cups coarsely chopped cranberries
1⅓ cups chopped walnuts, divided

Orange Honey Butter
½ cup (1 stick) butter, at room temp
2 tablespoons honey

1 tablespoon grated orange peel

Preheat oven to 350°F. Coat 18 muffin cups with no-stick cooking spray.

Combine flour, sugar, baking powder, nutmeg, cinnamon, baking soda, and ginger in a large mixing bowl. Cut in shortening with a pastry blender until mixture is the consistency of coarse crumbs. Combine eggs, orange peel, orange juice, and vanilla; stir into flour mixture just until ingredients are moistened. Gently stir in cranberries and about 1 cup of the nuts.

Spoon batter into prepared muffin cups. Sprinkle tops with remaining nuts. Bake for 25 to 30 minutes or until a wooden pick inserted near center comes out clean.

Combine butter, honey, and orange peel in a small mixer bowl; beat until fluffy.

Makes 18 muffins

Pumpkin Patch Muffins

Pumpkin muffins are always a treat when autumn approaches and warm, spicy foods have special appeal. A streusel topping or a sprinkling of nuts make these muffins special.

Ingredients

Streusel Topping

¼ cup firmly packed brown sugar
2 tablespoons all-purpose flour
1 tablespoon butter
½ teaspoon ground cinnamon
½ cup chopped nuts, if desired

Muffins

2 cups flour
1½ cups sugar
1½ teaspoons baking powder
½ teaspoon baking soda
½ teaspoon salt
1 teaspoon ground cinnamon
¼ teaspoon ground nutmeg
¼ teaspoon ground cloves
1 cup canned cooked pumpkin
⅓ cup vegetable oil
⅓ cup milk
2 eggs

Preheat oven to 350°F. Line 18 muffin cups with paper liners, or coat with no-stick cooking spray. Combine brown sugar, flour, butter, and cinnamon for streusel topping; blend with a fork until crumbly. Add nuts, if desired; set aside.

Combine flour, sugar, baking powder, baking soda, salt, and spices in a small bowl; set aside. Combine pumpkin, vegetable oil, milk, and eggs in a large mixing bowl; blend well. Add flour mixture and stir until blended. Spoon mixture into prepared muffin cups. Sprinkle with streusel topping. Bake 25 to 30 minutes or until a wooden pick inserted near center comes out clean.

Makes 18 muffins

CAROL'S TIDBITS

Chopped nuts or sunflower seeds are an optional topping instead of streusel.

Leftover pumpkin can be frozen for later use.

Almond
Coffee Cake

CAROL'S TIDBITS

Instead of the almond filling, combine 6 tablespoons granulated sugar, 1½ teaspoons ground cinnamon, and 1½ teaspoons vanilla extract in a small bowl; stir in ¾ cup chopped pecans. Sprinkle one-third of this mixture and ½ cup blueberries or ½ cup chocolate chips over each of three layers of batter. Bake as directed.

Tube pans are often referred to as angel food cake pans.

If you are a fan of almonds, this coffee cake is for you. A moist almond layer makes this coffee cake as delectable for dessert as for breakfast.

Ingredients

Almond Filling
4 tablespoons butter	1 cup powdered sugar
½ cup (3½ ounces) almond paste, crumbled	½ cup sliced almonds

Coffee Cake
1½ cups (3 sticks) butter, at room temp	3 cups flour
1½ cups granulated sugar	1½ teaspoons baking powder
3 eggs, at room temperature	1 teaspoon baking soda
1½ cups (12 ounces) dairy sour cream	1 teaspoon salt
1½ teaspoons vanilla extract	

Glaze
½ cup powdered sugar	¼ teaspoon vanilla extract
1 teaspoon butter, softened	1 to 2 teaspoons milk

Preheat oven to 375°F. Coat a 10-inch tube pan with no-stick cooking spray.

Melt butter for the filling in a small saucepan. Stir in almond paste and powdered sugar; cook over medium heat stirring constantly until smooth. Remove from heat and stir in almonds; set aside.

Beat butter and granulated sugar in a large mixer bowl until fluffy. Add eggs, one at a time, beating well on medium-high speed after each addition until light and creamy. Blend in sour cream and vanilla. Combine flour, baking powder, baking soda, and salt. Add to creamed mixture, blending on low speed just until smooth. Spread one-third of the batter in the prepared pan. Sprinkle with one-third of the filling. Repeat layering procedure twice. Bake 40 to 50 minutes or until a wooden pick inserted near the center comes out clean. Cool in pan for 20 minutes; remove from pan and cool on a wire rack.

Combine powdered sugar, butter, and vanilla in a small mixing bowl. Blend in enough milk to make a glaze consistency. Drizzle over cooled coffee cake.

Makes 1 coffee cake

Blueberry-Banana Bread

Blueberry and banana, two popular muffin flavors, share the spotlight in this delicious sweet bread. Try some of the other add-in options like cherries and chocolate chips.

Ingredients

1 cup sugar
6 tablespoons butter
2 eggs
1 cup mashed ripe bananas
   (about 3 medium bananas)
¼ cup milk

1 teaspoon vanilla extract
2 cups flour
1 teaspoon baking soda
½ teaspoon salt
½ cup coarsely chopped walnuts
1 cup fresh blueberries

Preheat oven to 350°F. Coat one 9x5-inch loaf pan, or three 5¾ x3¼-inch loaf pans with no-stick cooking spray; set aside.

Combine sugar and butter in a large mixer bowl; beat on high speed until fluffy. Beat in eggs until light and very creamy. Blend in bananas, milk, and vanilla on low speed. Stir in flour, baking soda, and salt. Stir in walnuts. Gently fold in blueberries. Spoon batter into prepared pan.

Bake 45 to 60 minutes or until a wooden pick inserted near center comes out clean. Cool in pan for 5 minutes; remove from pan and cool on wire rack.

Makes one large or three small loaves

CAROL'S TIDBITS

Extra ripe bananas are the secret to moist, sweet breads. If the bananas are ripe, but you do not have time to bake, just toss them in the freezer whole. They thaw enough to peel and mash in minutes.

Small blueberries are better than extra large. Frozen blueberries may be used; do not thaw before using.

Try other fruits and nuts like maraschino or dried cherries, dried or coarsely chopped fresh cranberries, raisins, chocolate pieces, pecans.

New England Brown Bread

CAROL'S TIDBITS

Bread can also be baked in a 9x5-inch loaf pan for 45 to 50 minutes.

I like Grandma's Original Molasses with the yellow lid whenever a recipe uses molasses.

Baking this bread in cans gives it a more interesting appearance.

This family favorite is known as "Can Bread" because I bake it in cans. It is a slightly sweet lowfat dark bread that I like to serve with soups and salads.

Ingredients

2 cups all-purpose flour
1½ cups whole wheat flour
½ cup firmly packed brown sugar
2 teaspoons baking soda

1 teaspoon salt
2 cups buttermilk
½ cup molasses

Preheat oven to 350°F. Coat the inside of five (14.5-ounce) vegetable/fruit cans with no-stick cooking spray. Place cans on a rimmed baking pan.

Combine flours, brown sugar, baking soda, and salt in a large mixing bowl. Stir in buttermilk and molasses; blend well. Spoon batter into prepared cans. Bake 40 to 45 minutes, or until a wooden pick inserted in center comes out clean. Cool bread in cans for 5 minutes; remove from cans and cool on a wire rack.

Makes 5 small loaves

Honey Raisin Brown Bread

CAROL'S TIDBITS

New England Brown Bread and Raisin Honey Wheat Brown Bread are very low in fat and high in flavor.

Add nuts instead of raisins, or use a mixture of both.

The ring shape from baking in a Bundt pan is fun but do not expect a very tall bread.

Serve this moist raisin bread with cream cheese for breakfast. Choose between baking it in a fluted tube pan for an interesting shape or in mini loaf pans.

Ingredients

2 cups whole wheat flour
1 cup all-purpose flour
2 teaspoons baking soda
1 cup raisins

2 cups buttermilk
½ cup honey
½ cup molasses

Preheat oven to 350°F. Coat a large Bundt pan or four 5¾ x3 x2¼-inch loaf pans with no-stick cooking spray.

Combine the flours, baking soda, and raisins in a large mixing bowl. Stir in buttermilk, honey, and molasses; blend well. Spoon batter into prepared pan. Bake bread in a Bundt pan for 45 to 50 minutes and in loaf pans for 35 to 40 minutes or until a wooden pick inserted near center comes out clean. Cool in pan for 5 minutes; remove from pan and cool on a wire rack.

Makes 1 Bundt ring bread or 4 mini loaves

Buttermilk Pancakes

Pancake mix has not been used in our house ever since my mother-in-law made these pancakes for us. We have them for brunch nearly every Sunday. Be sure to try the Maple Butter on them!

Ingredients

1 cup flour
1 tablespoon sugar
1 teaspoon baking powder
½ teaspoon baking soda

½ teaspoon salt
1¼ to 1½ cups buttermilk
2 tablespoons vegetable oil
1 egg

Combine flour, sugar, baking powder, baking soda, and salt in a medium mixing bowl; stir to blend. Combine buttermilk, vegetable oil, and egg; stir into dry ingredients just until blended.

Ladle batter onto lightly greased hot griddle using about ¼ cup batter per pancake. Cook until bubbles form on surface; turn to brown second side. Serve with Maple Butter or more traditional butter and syrup.

Makes 12 pancakes

Note: For thicker, fluffier pancakes, use lesser amount of buttermilk. For thinner, more dense pancakes, use larger amount of buttermilk.

Maple Butter

1 cup butter (not margarine/spread), at room temp
1 cup pure maple syrup

Beat butter in a small mixing bowl until creamed. Slowly beat in maple syrup until fluffy. If consistency is too soft or syrup separates from butter, beat in small amount of powdered sugar until desired consistency. Maple butter may be stored in refrigerator for several weeks.

Makes 1½ cups butter

CAROL'S TIDBITS

Since my mother-in-law measured by eye and feel, every family member has a slightly different written version of this recipe. I usually make the pancakes with half whole wheat flour and half all-purpose flour.

The first time I had maple butter was when a friend served it with French toast fondue in the '70s. We speared cubes of French bread into a cup of egg batter and then into the hot oil in the fondue pot. It was like eating a crispy French toast donut with a maple glaze. The sausage links were also cooked in the hot oil and were very crispy and succulent. Fresh peaches and blueberries with peach ice cream completed one of the most delicious and memorable breakfasts ever.

Pecan-Stuffed French Toast

CAROL'S TIDBITS

Any leftover filling makes a tasty spread on toasted bagels.

Nuts can be omitted in the filling or substituted with diced fresh strawberries.

This oven-baked French toast is a bed-and-breakfast specialty. Most of the preparation can be done the night before; bake it while the coffee brews.

Ingredients

1 package (8 ounces) cream cheese, softened
½ cup pecans, chopped
4 tablespoons sugar, divided
1½ teaspoons vanilla extract, divided
1 French bread baguette
3 eggs, lightly beaten

¾ cup milk
Dash salt
2 tablespoons butter, melted
2 tablespoons vegetable oil
1½ cups cornflake crumbs
Strawberry preserves, warmed
Powdered sugar

Combine cream cheese, pecans, 2 tablespoons of the sugar, and 1 teaspoon of the vanilla. Cut baguette on a bias into ½-inch-wide slices, cutting every other slice only ¾ of the way through. Spread about 1 tablespoon of the cream cheese filling in each slit; press closed. (Filled slices may be refrigerated overnight or frozen for up to 1 month; thaw frozen slices overnight in refrigerator.)

Preheat oven to 350°F. Combine eggs, milk, remaining 2 tablespoons sugar, remaining ½ teaspoon vanilla, and salt in a 9x13-inch baking dish. Dip baguette slices in egg mixture; turn and let slices set in egg mixture until all of the mixture is absorbed, about 10 minutes.

Combine melted butter and vegetable oil in a shallow 10x15-inch baking pan. Coat bread slices on all sides with cornflake crumbs; place in pan. Bake 10 minutes; turn slices and bake 8 to 10 additional minutes or until golden brown on bottom. Serve with warm strawberry preserves and a dusting of powdered sugar.

Makes 6 servings

Pecan Cornbread Sticks with Honey Butter

Cornbread takes on a new flavor by adding pecans and a new shape by cutting into thin breadsticks. Crispy and delicious with Honey Butter!

Ingredients

6 tablespoons butter
1 cup flour
1 cup cornmeal
⅓ cup sugar
1 tablespoon baking powder

1 teaspoon salt
1 cup milk
2 eggs
⅓ cup finely chopped pecans

Honey Butter
½ cup (1 stick) butter, at room temp

¼ cup honey

Preheat oven to 425°F. Place butter in a 9x13-inch baking pan; heat in oven until butter is melted, about 3 minutes.

Combine flour, cornmeal, sugar, baking powder, and salt in a mixing bowl. Combine milk and eggs in a 2-cup glass measure; stir into flour mixture, blending with a whisk until nearly smooth. Stir in pecans and melted butter from baking pan. Pour batter into baking pan; bake 15 to 20 or minutes until crust is golden brown. Cool cornbread in pan 5 minutes. Turn cornbread out onto cutting board; cut in half lengthwise and crosswise into 1-inch-wide cornbread sticks.

Beat butter with mixer or food processor until fluffy. Gradually beat in honey until well blended. Serve with warm cornbread sticks.

Makes 24 cornbread sticks

CAROL'S TIDBITS

Cornbread batter can also be baked as mini muffins. Brush 24 mini muffin cups with melted butter; add remaining butter to batter. Fill muffin cups; bake 12 to 15 minutes.

Melting butter in the pan makes a crispy, buttery crust.

Buttermilk Biscuits

CAROL'S TIDBITS

If making biscuits with regular milk, increase baking powder to 1 tablespoon and omit baking soda. The dough will be more moist and may need a little extra flour added when shaping the dough into a ball.

Use buttermilk for the best tasting and lightest textured biscuits!

Self-rising flour, a soft wheat flour with baking powder and salt already added, was used by most Southern bakers. 2 cups self-rising flour = 2 cups all purpose flour, 1 tablespoon baking powder, and ½ teaspoon salt.

The women I observed making biscuits felt that using self-rising flour and solid vegetable shortening were the two most important ingredients in biscuits.

Long, ½-inch high sticks were placed next to the biscuit dough to use as a guide for consistent height when the biscuits were baked for consumer tests.

Much of my career at The Pillsbury Company in Minneapolis was spent working with refrigerated biscuit products. The South was known for their melt-in-your-mouth, tasty biscuits made fresh for every meal so I was off to do research. I had the wonderful experience of watching scratch bakers throughout the South make biscuits in their own kitchens and tasting them hot out of the oven. What a treat! This is a buttermilk version that I like to serve with butter and honey.

Ingredients

2 cups all-purpose flour
2 teaspoons baking powder
½ teaspoon baking soda

½ teaspoon salt
½ cup solid vegetable shortening
¾ cup buttermilk

Preheat oven to 450°F. Combine flour, baking powder, baking soda, and salt in a large mixing bowl; cut in shortening with a pastry blender until the consistency of coarse meal with some pieces the size of small peas. Stir in buttermilk.

Turn dough out onto a lightly floured surface and gently form into a ball that is no longer sticky. Flatten dough to about ¾ inch and cut into biscuits with a 2-inch biscuit cutter.

Place biscuits on a parchment-lined baking sheet. For tall, fluffy biscuits, place biscuits close together; for short, crispy biscuits, bake biscuits about 2-inches apart on the baking sheet. Bake 12 to 15 minutes or until golden brown.

Makes 12 biscuits

Carol Meyer's Scratch Biscuits

This is a Southern version of "take-two-and-butter-them-while-hot" biscuits used as a control in consumer tests. I was given a plaque with this recipe when I left Pillsbury. It has been on display in my kitchen ever since.

2 cups self-rising flour
½ cup solid vegetable shortening

¾ cup milk

Preheat oven to 450°F. Sift flour. Cut in shortening with fork 'till consistency of coarse meal. Quickly stir in milk. Mix 'till soft, moist, and porous. Turn onto a floured surface, sprinkle dough lightly with flour; knead 'till dough is no longer sticky. Flatten with hand to almost desired thickness. Place measuring sticks around dough. Roll out to desired height. Cut with a floured 2-inch cutter. Bake on an ungreased cookie sheet, at 450°F for 12 to 15 minutes, 'till golden brown.

Makes 12 biscuits

Note: If using all-purpose flour, add 1 tablespoon baking powder and ½ teaspoon salt.

Cheese and
Green Onion Biscuits

These biscuits are pretty hard to resist . . . just like those served in many restaurants with soups and salads.

Ingredients

1½ cups flour
½ cup yellow cornmeal
2 teaspoons baking powder
½ teaspoon baking soda
½ teaspoon seasoned salt
4 tablespoons cold butter, cubed

1 cup (4 ounces) shredded sharp
  Cheddar cheese
¼ cup grated Parmesan cheese
¼ cup chopped green onions
1¼ cups buttermilk

Preheat oven to 450°F. Line a baking sheet with parchment paper.

Combine flour, cornmeal, baking powder, baking soda, and salt in a mixing bowl. Cut in butter with a pastry blender until butter is the size of small peas. Add **cheeses and onion; toss to mix.** Stir in buttermilk. Drop dough, **about 3** tablespoons per biscuit, onto prepared baking sheet. Bake 12 to 15 minutes or until biscuits are golden brown.

Makes 16 biscuits

CAROL'S TIDBITS

Brush melted butter over baked biscuits for extra rich, buttery biscuits.

Mini biscuits make great appetizers. Use 1 tablespoon dough for each biscuit; bake 8 to 10 minutes.

Pimiento Cheese Breadsticks

CAROL'S TIDBITS

Cut bread into larger pieces for an open-face sandwich.

The spread can also be served on crackers or crostini.

Prepared breadsticks may be frozen before baking. Bake frozen breadsticks 15 to 18 minutes.

For a popular taste of the South, pimiento cheese spread turns French bread into crispy, cheesy breadsticks. Great with a BBQ or as an appetizer.

Ingredients

1 loaf (16 ounces) French bread
½ cup mayonnaise
½ cup chopped onion
1 jar (2 ounces) chopped pimiento, drained

2 tablespoons chopped fresh parsley
1 teaspoon dry mustard
¼ teaspoon garlic powder
2 cups (8 ounces) shredded sharp Cheddar cheese

Preheat oven to 400°F. Line a baking sheet with parchment paper or foil. Slice bread horizontally into 3 slices and place on the baking sheet.

Combine mayonnaise, onion, pimiento, parsley, dry mustard, and garlic powder in a mixing bowl. Stir in cheese; blend well. Spread mixture over bread slices. Cut each slice crosswise into 16 sticks. Bake 10 to 12 minutes or until cheese is bubbly and golden brown.

Makes 48 sticks

Garlic Herb Baguette Breadsticks

CAROL'S TIDBITS

For more crispy breadsticks, separate breadsticks slightly before baking. For softer breadsticks, bake breadsticks with sides touching.

I love the fun shape and texture of breadsticks made from a French bread baguette. Use your favorite seasonings and cheese to make these quick and easy breadsticks.

Ingredients

1 French bread baguette
4 tablespoons butter, melted
2 tablespoons olive oil
2 tablespoons minced green onion
1 clove garlic, minced

¼ teaspoon rosemary, thyme, or basil, crushed
Dash cayenne pepper
1 cup (4 ounces) shredded Asiago cheese

Preheat oven to 400°F. Line a baking sheet with parchment paper or foil.

Cut the baguette in half both crosswise and lengthwise. Then cut each piece lengthwise into thirds to make 12 breadsticks. Arrange breadsticks close together on the prepared baking sheet. Combine melted butter, olive oil, green onion, garlic, herb, and cayenne; brush over cut surface of each breadstick and sprinkle with cheese. Bake 7 to 10 minutes or until golden brown.

Makes 12 breadsticks

Herb Focaccia

It is easy to make this Italian flat bread using a food processor. Add toppings of your choice: simple herbs and salt, sliced tomatoes, onions, and olives.

Ingredients

¼ cup very hot water

1 teaspoon dried or fresh rosemary leaves

1 package (.25 ounce) active dry yeast

1 teaspoon sugar

3 cups unbleached bread flour

1 teaspoon salt

½ teaspoon crushed red pepper flakes

5 to 6 tablespoons extra virgin olive oil, divided

½ to ¾ cup water

1 to 3 teaspoons chopped rosemary or other herbs

Coarse salt

Freshly grated Parmesan cheese

Steep the 1 teaspoon rosemary in hot water until water is cooled to 105°-110°F. Strain rosemary from water, reserving water; discard rosemary. Stir yeast and sugar into water; let stand until bubbly.

Combine flour, salt, and red pepper flakes in a food processor work bowl fitted with steel knife blade; pulse to blend ingredients. Add 2 tablespoons olive oil to yeast mixture. With machine running, slowly add yeast to flour mixture; follow with enough remaining water until dough forms a ball. Process 30 seconds. Place dough in a bowl coated with no-stick cooking spray; cover with plastic wrap and let rise 45 minutes.

Coat a large baking sheet with no-stick cooking spray. Press dough into a flat sheet on the pan. Loosely cover dough and let rise until dough begins to rise.

Preheat oven to 400°F. Press indentations into dough with fingers. Drizzle remaining olive oil over dough; sprinkle with herbs, salt, and Parmesan. Add optional toppings, if desired. Bake 15 to 20 minutes.

Makes one focaccia (about 10x12-inches)

CAROL'S TIDBITS

Optional toppings: Thinly sliced Roma tomatoes, red onion, ripe or kalamata olives, artichoke hearts, goat cheese, etc.

Cut baked focaccia into squares; split and add your favorite sandwich makings.

Super Easy
Make-Ahead Croissants

CAROL'S TIDBITS

If using rapid-rising yeast, heat water, milk, and 4 table- spoons butter to 120°-130°F. Combine with yeast, sugar, salt, and 1½ cups of the flour; whisk until smooth. Let mixture stand 20 minutes; whisk in egg. Continue, beginning with combining remaining 4 cups of the flour.

Up to 2½ cups whole wheat flour may be substituted for the all-purpose flour.

Dough can be used for sweet rolls and coffee cakes.

Thanksgiving and other holiday dinners would not be complete without baskets of these warm yeast rolls. The dough can also be used to make cinnamon and caramel rolls.

Ingredients

1 cup warm (105°-115°F) water
2 packages (.25 ounce each) active dry yeast
Pinch sugar
⅔ cup milk
4 tablespoons butter, melted
1 egg

⅓ cup sugar
1½ teaspoons salt
5½ cups all-purpose or unbleached flour, divided
1 cup (2 sticks) butter, chilled and cubed
Melted butter, if desired

Combine yeast and water with a pinch of sugar in a large mixing bowl; let stand until bubbly. Whisk in milk, melted butter, egg, sugar, salt, and 1½ cups of the flour; whisk until smooth and set aside.

Combine remaining 4 cups of the flour and the cold butter in a food processor work bowl. Pulse until butter pieces are no larger than the size of peas. Stir flour mixture into batter in large bowl just until moistened. Cover dough with plastic wrap and refrigerate until thoroughy chilled, 4 hours or up to 2 days.

Turn dough out onto floured surface and knead about 6 times until dough forms a smooth ball. Divide dough into 4 parts; roll each part into a circle about ¼ inch thick. Cut dough into 8 pie-shaped wedges. Starting with the wide end, roll up each wedge toward point. Place rolls on an ungreased baking sheet and curve ends to form crescent shapes. Cover rolls loosely with a clean towel. Let rolls rise until doubled in size, about 1 to 1½ hours.

Preheat oven to 350°F. Bake rolls 20 to 25 minutes or until golden brown. Brush warm rolls with melted butter for a soft, shiny crust.

Makes 32 rolls

Cherry Cheese Stollen

This is a great coffee bread for Christmas morning or a Valentine's Day brunch. Make and shape the dough the night before to bake in the morning. Use half of the dough for a stollen and the other half for a small pan of caramel or cinnamon rolls.

Ingredients

Dough
4 to 4½ cups all-purpose or
   unbleached flour, divided
⅓ cup sugar
½ teaspoon salt
1 package (.25 ounce) rapid-rising
   dry yeast

¾ cup milk
¼ cup water
8 tablespoons butter, cubed
1 egg
1 can (30 ounces) cherry pie filling

Filling
2 packages (8 ounces each) cream
   cheese, softened
½ cup sugar

1 teaspoon almond or 2 teaspoons
   vanilla extract
Dash salt

Combine 2 cups of the flour with sugar, salt, and yeast in a large mixer bowl. Combine milk, water, and butter in a small saucepan; heat to 120°-130°F (butter may not be completely melted). Add to flour mixture and beat with paddle attachment on medium speed until smooth. Add egg and beat on high speed for 3 minutes. Gradually add enough of the remaining flour on low speed until dough begins to cling to beater and come away from the sides of the bowl.

Replace paddle attachment with dough hook. Knead dough on low speed, adding flour as necessary, for 3 to 4 minutes or until smooth and satiny. Turn dough out onto a lightly floured surface and knead into a smooth, round ball. Place dough in a large bowl coated with no-stick cooking spray, rolling the dough around the bowl to coat with spray. Cover bowl with plastic wrap and let rise in a warm place until doubled in size, about 1½ to 2 hours.

Combine cream cheese, sugar, almond extract, and salt in a mixer bowl; beat until fluffy. Divide dough in half. Roll one half into 14x12-inch rectangle on a lightly floured surface. Spread half of the cream cheese filling over dough, leaving 1-inch border on all sides. Starting with one 12-inch side, roll dough jellyroll-style to center; repeat with other 12-inch side. Transfer to a baking sheet coated with no-stick cooking spray. Cut slits through rolled sides to center with scissors or knife. Repeat shaping with other portion of dough. Let dough rise, covered, for 1 hour or until doubled in size.

Preheat oven to 350°F. Bake stollens for 25 to 30 minutes or until golden brown. Spoon half of the cherry pie filling down center of each warm stollen. Drizzle with glaze.

Makes 2 stollens

*This recipe, or the cute picture of our young sons, caught the reader's attention when it was published in a "Cook of the Week" feature in the **St. Louis Post Dispatch**. It was selected as one of the reader's favorite recipes of that year and later included in **The Best Recipes Cookbook**, a 21-year collection of favorite recipes printed in the newspaper.*

To make ahead, shape dough and let rise 20 minutes. Cover with foil to keep air out but do not let foil touch dough; refrigerate overnight. In the morning, let dough rise at room temperature for about 1 hour before baking.

For glaze: combine 1½ cups powdered sugar, 1 tablespoon soft butter, and 1 teaspoon almond extract or vanilla in a bowl until blended. Gradually add enough milk to make a smooth glaze; drizzle over slightly warm stollens.

Caramel Rolls

CAROL'S TIDBITS

Use dental floss to cut the rolled up dough into individual rolls. Slip a 12-inch length of dental floss under the rolled up dough where dough should be sliced, cross the ends and pull tightly.

For larger rolls, roll dough into 16x12-inch rectangles and spread with filling. Roll up starting with a 12-inch side. Cut dough into 12 rolls.

They use to say that the way to a man's heart was thru his stomach. Lyle loves caramel rolls and I used this recipe to win his heart when we were dating. I worked in The Pillsbury Kitchens located across the street from his office and occasionally used the ovens to bake caramel rolls that had been shaped the night before. Fresh from the oven, gooey caramel rolls would arrive just in time for his office's coffee break. I hoped his co-workers would put pressure on him to make that a permanent arrangement. We have been married 40 years!

Ingredients

Dough

¼ cup warm (105°-115°F) water
1 package (.25 ounce) active dry yeast
Pinch of granulated sugar
¾ cup milk
6 tablespoons butter, cut up

3¾ to 4 cups all-purpose or unbleached flour, divided
⅓ cup granulated sugar
½ teaspoon salt
1 egg

Caramel Topping

½ cup (1 stick) butter
½ cup firmly packed brown sugar

1 tablespoon light corn syrup
1 cup coarsely chopped pecans

Filling

2 tablespoons butter, softened
2 tablespoons granulated sugar

2 tablespoons brown sugar
½ teaspoon ground cinnamon

Combine water, yeast, and a pinch of sugar in a large mixer bowl; let stand until bubbly. Heat milk and butter in a small saucepan over medium heat until 105°-115°F (butter might not be melted). Add warm milk, 2 cups of the flour, sugar, and salt to yeast mixture; beat until smooth. Add egg and beat on medium speed for 3 minutes. Gradually add enough remaining flour to form a soft dough.

Knead dough by hand on a lightly floured surface for 5 to 10 minutes, or for 3 minutes with mixer fitted with dough hook on lowest speed. Place dough in a bowl coated with no-stick cooking spray; cover with plastic wrap and let rise until doubled in size, about 1½ to 2 hours.

Combine butter, brown sugar, and corn syrup for topping in a small saucepan; cook over medium heat until butter melts and sugar is nearly dissolved (do not boil). Stir mixture to blend ingredients until smooth. Pour into an ungreased 9x13-inch baking pan; sprinkle with pecans.

Continued next page

Roll dough on a lightly floured surface into a 20x10-inch rectangle. Spread softened butter over the dough; sprinkle with a mixture of sugars and cinnamon. Roll up dough, starting with a 20-inch side. Cut rolled dough into 20 slices; place cut-side down over caramel topping. Cover rolls with plastic wrap and let rise until doubled, about 45 to 60 minutes.

Preheat oven to 375°F. Bake rolls 25 to 30 minutes or until golden brown. Remove rolls from oven and cool 1 minute. Invert pan onto a tray; let stand 1 minute before removing pan to allow topping to drip onto rolls.

Makes 20 rolls

Cinnamon Rolls

Use the same dough recipe to shape rolls with a buttery cinnamon filling. Drizzle the baked rolls with a vanilla glaze.

Ingredients

1 recipe Caramel Roll dough

Filling

2 tablespoons butter, softened

2 tablespoons granulated sugar

2 tablespoons brown sugar

1 tablespoon ground cinnamon

½ to 1 cup raisins, if desired

Glaze

1 cup powdered sugar

1 tablespoon butter, softened

1 teaspoon vanilla extract

About 2 tablespoons milk

Prepare dough according to Caramel Rolls directions.

Roll dough into a 20x10-inch rectangle and spread with butter, leaving a 1-inch border along one 20-inch side. Sprinkle with mixture of sugars and cinnamon; sprinkle with raisins. Roll up dough toward edge without butter. Cut into 20 rolls. Place rolls in a 9x13-inch baking pan coated with no-stick cooking spray. Cover and let rise until doubled in size, about 45 to 60 minutes.

Preheat oven to 375°F. Bake 25 to 30 minutes or until golden brown. Cool slightly. Combine powdered sugar, butter, and vanilla in a small bowl. Stir in enough milk to make smooth consistency. Drizzle over warm rolls.

Makes 20 rolls

CAROL'S TIDBITS

For flat, crispy cinnamon rolls, bake rolls on a baking sheet coated with no-stick cooking spray. Bake until golden, about 20 minutes.

Maple-Nut Coffee Twist

CAROL'S TIDBITS

For a great springtime coffee cake, substitute freshly grated orange peel for the maple flavoring in the dough, filling, and glaze; also use orange juice instead of milk in the glaze.

For a cinnamon coffee cake, omit maple flavoring in dough, filling, and glaze; increase cinnamon to 1 tablespoon in the filling and add ¼ teaspoon vanilla extract to glaze.

This was one of my favorite recipes to make in my early bread baking classes. A no-knead dough is shaped into a coffee cake with pull-apart wedges that is fun to make and even better to eat.

Ingredients

Dough
3 to 3½ cups all-purpose or unbleached flour, divided
¼ cup granulated sugar
1 teaspoon salt
1 package (.25 ounce) rapid-rising dry yeast

1 cup milk
4 tablespoons butter, cut into small pieces
1 egg, at room temp
1 teaspoon maple flavoring

Filling
3 tablespoons butter, melted
½ cup granulated sugar
1 teaspoon ground cinnamon

1 teaspoon maple flavoring
⅓ cup finely chopped pecans or walnuts

Glaze
1 cup powdered sugar
1 tablespoon butter, softened

¼ teaspoon maple flavoring
About 2 tablespoons milk

Combine 1 cup of the flour, sugar, salt, and yeast in a large mixer bowl. Combine milk and butter in a small saucepan and heat to 120°-130°F. Add to flour mixture and beat until moistened. Add egg and beat on medium speed for 3 minutes. Gradually add enough remaining flour to form a soft dough. Cover and let rise until doubled in size, about 1 to 1½ hours.

Turn dough out onto a floured surface and knead until no longer sticky. Divide dough into 3 balls. Roll 1 ball into a 12-inch circle and fit into bottom of a 12-inch pizza pan coated with no-stick cooking spray. Brush dough with 1 tablespoon of the melted butter. Combine sugar, cinnamon, and maple flavoring; mix until blended. Stir in nuts; sprinkle ⅓ of the mixture over dough. Repeat procedure with remaining dough balls, butter and sugar mixture. Set a 2-inch glass in the center of the dough. Use scissors to cut from outside edge just to the glass, forming 16 pie-shaped wedges. Twist each wedge 4 times; remove glass. Cover and let rise until doubled in size, about 30 to 45 minutes.

Preheat oven to 375°F. Bake coffee cake 20 to 25 minutes or until golden brown. Combine powdered sugar, butter, maple flavoring, and enough milk to make a smooth glaze. Drizzle over warm coffee cake.

Makes 1 coffee cake

ENTRÉES

From weekday family favorites to
special occasion entrees, these savory
main courses will be the star of the meal.

Blackberry-Glazed Tenderloin of Pork

Simply elegant! A delicious two-ingredient sauce and a garnish of fresh blackberries and rosemary makes this a perfect entrée for any occasion.

Ingredients

2 pork tenderloins (about 1 pound each)
½ cup olive oil
2 tablespoons chopped fresh rosemary
1½ teaspoons dried leaf or rubbed sage

1 teaspoon salt
½ teaspoon freshly ground black pepper
1 tablespoon olive oil
Fresh blackberries
Rosemary sprigs

Glaze
¾ cup (10 ounces) seedless blackberry or black raspberry jam

¼ cup sweet vermouth

Trim tenderloins and place in a large freezer-weight reclosable plastic bag. Whisk the ½ cup olive oil, rosemary, sage, salt, and pepper in a 2-cup glass measure; pour over tenderloins. Seal bag and turn to coat meat; refrigerate for 2 to 4 hours.

Preheat oven to 400°F. Remove tenderloins from marinade and pat dry with paper towel; discard marinade. Heat olive oil in a large skillet over medium-high heat. Add tenderloins and sear all sides until lightly browned. Transfer tenderloins to rack in a shallow roasting pan and roast until internal temperature of 150°F, about 20 to 25 minutes. Cover with foil and let rest for 10 minutes before slicing.

Combine jam and vermouth in a small saucepan. Warm over low heat stirring often until smooth and slightly thickened.

Serve sliced tenderloins with slightly warm glaze and garnish with fresh rosemary and blackberries.

Makes 6 servings

CAROL'S TIDBITS

Searing the tenderloin before baking adds caramel flavor and color to the outside. If tenderloin is roasted without searing, brush with 2 to 4 tablespoons of the glaze the last 10 minutes of roasting.

Rubbed sage is crumbled dried sage and is less powdery than ground sage.

Red raspberry jam, apricot preserves, or peach preserves can be substituted for the black raspberry jam.

Serve with Puréed Sweet Potatoes (page 137) and Green Beens with Toasted Garlic Butter Crumbs (page 132) .

Pork Loin Roasts

CAROL'S TIDBITS

Pork loin roasts are always a popular choice because they are very easy to prepare and serve. They can look impressive and taste totally different depending on the seasonings, glazes, and sauces served with the roasts.

The secret to a great pork roast is not overcooking it. The USDA recommends cooking pork to an internal temperature of 145°F, but most of my students prefer it to be 150° to 155°F. It will be slightly pink in the center, juicy, tender, and very flavorful. It is important to cover the roast with foil and let it stand for 5 to 10 minutes after cooking to allow the juices to be absorbed into the meat. The temperature will rise about 5°F.

I highly recommend using probe thermometers when roasting any meat. The thermometer inserted into the center of a roast before putting it into the oven is connected to a display outside the oven. The display can be set to the desired end temperature. The temperature can be monitored as the roast cooks; an alert will be sounded when the temperature is reached. Using a probe thermometer eliminates frequent opening of the oven which affects the roasting temperature and time. It also eliminates loss of meat juices from repeated piercing with an instant-read thermometer. Avoid touching bones with the probe as it may give a false reading.

Some pork cuts (loin roasts, chops, ribs, and shoulder roasts) benefit from optional brining which imparts flavor and moisture into the meat. The brine contains both salt and sugar; herbs and spices can be added. Brining does not benefit tenderloins.

Brine Solution for Pork

Ingredients

2 cups hot water	1 tablespoon molasses
¼ cup firmly packed brown sugar	2 cups ice water
¼ cup kosher salt	

Combine hot water, brown sugar, salt, and molasses in a large bowl; stir until sugar and salt are dissolved. Stir in ice water and cool to room temperature or colder.

Place roast in a large, freezer-weight reclosable plastic bag and add cooled brine solution. Squeeze out air; seal bag and also tie with tie twist to keep roast covered with brine. Place roast in a 9x13-inch pan; refrigerate for 4 to 6 hours. After brining, remove roast and pat dry with paper towels. Roast following recipe directions.

Pork Loin Roast with Soy-Laced Peach & Ginger Sauce

Sweet, salty, smoky, fruity, all combined into one sauce with an Asian flair. You will love it! Make the sauce ahead and store extra in the freezer for serving with chops or tenderloin.

Ingredients

1 boneless pork loin roast
(3 to 4 pounds)

Brine, if desired or coarse salt
Freshly ground black pepper

Soy-Laced Peach & Ginger Sauce

1 tablespoon toasted sesame oil
½ cup slivered shallots
2 cloves garlic, minced
1½ teaspoons minced fresh ginger
1 jar (18 ounces) peach preserves
2 tablespoons less sodium soy sauce

2 tablespoons rice wine vinegar
1 tablespoon julienned fresh ginger
1½ teaspoons ground coriander
seed, or 2 teaspoons coriander
seed, coarsely cracked

CAROL'S TIDBITS

Cooled peach sauce may be stored in a covered container in refrigerator (or longer if frozen) but flavor is most intense when freshly made. Boost the flavor with additional julienned fresh ginger.

Coriander seed adds a spark of lemon, sage, and caraway to the sauce. Although it is the seed of the cilantro plant, there is no similarity in flavor.

Brine roast, if desired (page 100). Pat dry with paper towels; season with salt and pepper. Omit salt if roast was brined.

Preheat oven to 350°F. Place roast on a rack in a shallow roasting pan. Roast 45 minutes before adding sauce.

For the sauce: Cook shallots, garlic, and minced ginger in sesame oil in a medium saucepan over medium heat stirring often until shallots are lightly caramelized, about 8 minutes. Stir in peach preserves. Increase heat to high; bring to a boil, stirring often. Remove from heat; stir in soy sauce, vinegar, julienned ginger, and coriander.

Remove 4 tablespoons of the sauce and spoon over roast. Continue to roast until internal temperature is 150°F, about 20 to 40 minutes. Cover loosely with foil and let rest for 10 minutes before slicing. Serve with warm Soy-Laced Peach & Ginger Sauce.

Makes 10 to 12 servings

Pork Loin Roast
with Orange Honey Glaze

CAROL'S TIDBITS

Orange Honey Glaze is excellent on roasted sweet potatoes. Either glaze is delicious with pork tenderloin or chops.

Be sure to use pure maple syrup, not maple-flavored pancake syrup which is very sweet. Pure maple syrup must be refrigerated after opening.

Use a small light-colored roasting pan to keep drippings from getting too brown. Add water to drippings if becoming too brown.

This is a good choice for an Easter dinner or other springtime occasion. The glaze is also good on ham.

Ingredients

1 boneless pork loin roast
  (3 to 4 pounds)

Brine, if desired or coarse salt
Freshly ground black pepper

Orange Honey Glaze
¾ cup honey
½ cup dark brown sugar

2 teaspoons grated orange peel
½ cup orange juice

Brine roast, if desired (page 100). Pat dry with paper towels; season with salt and pepper. Omit salt if roast was brined.

Preheat oven to 350 °F. Place roast on rack in a shallow roasting pan. Roast 45 minutes before brushing with glaze.

For the glaze: Combine honey, brown sugar, orange peel, and juice in a small saucepan; cook over medium heat stirring often until sugar is dissolved and sauce has syrup consistency.

Remove 4 tablespoons of the glaze and brush over roast. Roast 20 to 40 additional minutes until internal temperature of 150 °F. Cover roast loosely with foil and let rest for 10 minutes before slicing. Serve with remaining warm Orange Honey Glaze.

Makes 10 to 12 servings

Pork Loin Roast with Maple Dijon Glaze: Prepare roast as above substituting a mixture of 1 cup pure maple syrup and ⅓ cup Dijon mustard for Orange Honey Glaze. Brush partially-baked roast with 2 to 4 tablespoons of the mixture. Roast 20 to 40 additional minutes until 150˚F. Stir remaining Dijon mixture into juices in roasting pan; heat over medium heat until the consistency of syrup. Strain and serve with sliced roast.

Caribbean Grilled Ribs

Spicy, sweet, and hot (but not too hot) describes the jerk seasoning used to season these ribs. You will love the dipping sauce for these ribs!

Ingredients

Jerk Seasoning
2 tablespoons onion powder
2 teaspoons coarse salt
2 teaspoons coarse ground black pepper
2 teaspoons ground allspice

1 teaspoon dried thyme
1 teaspoon freshly grated nutmeg
1 teaspoon cayenne pepper
½ teaspoon ground cinnamon

Ribs
4 pounds pork loin baby back ribs
¼ cup less sodium soy sauce
2 tablespoons vegetable oil

1 tablespoon white vinegar
Jerk seasoning, divided

Honey Soy Sauce
1 tablespoon Jerk Seasoning
1 tablespoon cornstarch
½ cup water

⅓ cup less sodium soy sauce
⅓ cup honey
¼ cup red wine vinegar

Combine all jerk seasoning ingredients in a small bowl; blend well and set aside.

Loosen tough membrane covering back of ribs by sliding a sharp knife under membrane at one end of slab. Use a paper towel to firmly grasp loosened membrane; quickly pull membrane off. Place ribs in a 2-gallon freezer-weight reclosable plastic bag. Combine the ¼ cup soy sauce, vegetable oil, white vinegar, and 2 tablespoons of the jerk seasoning; pour over ribs. Marinate in refrigerator for at least 3 hours or overnight.

Combine 1 tablespoon of the jerk seasoning and cornstarch in a small saucepan; stir in water until cornstarch is dissolved. Stir in the ⅓ cup soy sauce, honey, and red vinegar. Cook sauce over medium heat stirring often until sauce thickens. Pour ½ cup sauce into a small bowl for basting ribs; reserve remaining sauce to serve warm or at room temperature as a dipping sauce with the ribs.

Preheat grill to high for 15 minutes. Remove ribs from marinade (discard marinade) and pat dry with a paper towel. Rub surface with remaining jerk seasoning. Turn grill burners off under grid where ribs will sit; turn other burners to medium (300°F). Grill ribs over indirect heat turning often until ribs are tender, about 1½ hours. Brush ribs with ½ cup Honey Soy Sauce during last 20 minutes of cooking. Cut ribs into serving pieces and serve with reserved Honey Soy Sauce.

Makes 4 servings

CAROL'S TIDBITS

Allow 1 pound ribs per serving.

Jerk seasoning is a mix of sweet, spicy, and hot. A key ingredient is ground allspice, known as ground Jamaican pepper (pimento). Allspice is the pea-size berry of the evergreen pimento tree native to the West Indies and South America, but primarily Jamaica. It tastes like a combination of cinnamon, nutmeg, and cloves and is used in sweet and savory cooking.

If hotter seasoning is desired, increase levels of pepper, particularly the cayenne pepper.

Make a quantity of jerk seasoning to keep on hand to use on pork, chicken, and fish.

Grilled Pork Chops with Apricot Glaze

CAROL'S TIDBITS

Chops need to be at least 1 inch thick to get a nicely browned outside and a tender, moist inside.

Familiar pork cuts are sporting newer names. Ribeye chops were rib chops; New York pork chops were boneless top loin chops; porterhouse pork chops were bone-in loin chops.

An apricot glaze with Asian seasonings can be used on either boneless or bone-in chops. Be sure to add the sprinkling of chopped peanuts and green onion for the finishing touch.

Ingredients

6 to 8 pork chops (1-inch thick)
Vegetable oil
2 teaspoons ground ginger
1 teaspoon coarse salt
½ teaspoon garlic powder
½ teaspoon seasoned pepper

1 cup apricot preserves
¼ cup hoison sauce
½ teaspoon crushed red pepper flakes
Chopped peanuts and/or thinly sliced green onion

Brush pork chops with vegetable oil. Combine ginger, salt, garlic powder, and seasoned pepper in a small bowl; rub mixture over both sides of chops.

Combine apricot preserves, hoison sauce, and pepper flakes in a small saucepan; cook over medium heat stirring often until preserves are melted. Pour half of the mixture in a small bowl for basting and reserve remaining glaze to serve with grilled chops.

Preheat grill to medium-high. Place chops on oiled grill grid; cover and grill for 4 minutes. Turn chops; brush grilled surface with apricot glaze. Grill second side for 4 minutes; turn and brush with glaze. Grill until internal temperature of 145°F and glaze is caramelized, about 1 to 2 additional minutes.

Sprinkle chopped peanuts and/or sliced green onions over chops. Serve with reserved apricot glaze.

Makes 6 to 8 servings

104

Peppered Beef Medallions with Blackberry Port Sauce

I was inspired to make this recipe after enjoying a very similar entrée made with elk. Since elk is not readily available in most markets, I developed the recipe using beef petite shoulder tender roasts. Beef tenderloin filets would make the entrée even more divine.

Ingredients

Blackberry Port Sauce

1 carton (6 ounces) blackberries
1 cup ruby port wine
3 to 4 tablespoons sugar

2 sprigs fresh thyme
⅛ to ¼ teaspoon crushed red pepper flakes

Beef Medallions

1½ pounds beef petite shoulder tender roasts
Olive or vegetable oil

Coarse salt
Freshly ground black pepper

For sauce: Combine blackberries, port wine, 3 tablespoons sugar, thyme, and pepper flakes in a small saucepan; bring to a boil over medium-high heat. Reduce heat and simmer, uncovered, stirring occasionally for 30 minutes. Remove and discard thyme sprigs. Press mixture thru a mesh sieve to remove seeds; discard seeds. Add remaining sugar to taste. Return sauce to saucepan and cook until sauce is syrup consistency. (Sauce may be made ahead and refrigerated; reheat before serving.)

For medallions: Cut roasts into 6 medallions. Butterfly each medallion by cutting almost in half. Open medallions and shape into filets. Insert a wooden toothpick at base of each to prevent opening while cooking. Brush medallions with oil and season with salt and pepper. Heat small amount of oil in a medium skillet over medium-high heat. Add medallions and cook for 3 to 4 minutes on each side until browned. Transfer meat to platter; cover with foil and let rest for 5 minutes before serving with Blackberry Port Sauce.

Makes 4 to 6 servings

CAROL'S TIDBITS

Ruby port wine is a fortified wine from Portugal and has a berry-like flavor. Fortified wine is wine with added spirits like brandy; opened bottles have a longer shelf life than regular wine.

Serve the medallions with a garnish of asparagus spears, green beans, and red and yellow pepper strips brushed with olive oil, seasoned with salt and herbs, and then roasted at 425 °F for 10 to 12 minutes.

Beef petite shoulder tender roasts are available already cut into medallions. I prefer cutting the medallions to insure more uniformity.

Beef Tenderloin with Marsala-Mushroom Sauce

Beef tenderloin is a special occasion meat and it deserves an equally special sauce. Marsala, a fortified wine from Sicily, adds a smoky richness to the mushroom sauce. The sauce is also delicious on beef petite shoulder tenders.

Ingredients

3 pounds trimmed center-cut beef tenderloin
Olive oil

Coarse salt
Freshly ground black pepper

Marsala-Mushroom Sauce

2 tablespoons butter
1 cup sliced leeks
3 large cloves garlic, minced
2 cups sliced baby bella mushrooms, about 6 ounces
2 cups sliced shiitake mushroom caps, about 6 ounces

1 cup dry Marsala wine
1 cup (8 ounces) beef stock
2 tablespoons chilled butter, cubed
Coarse salt
Freshly ground black pepper

Preheat oven to 425°F. Rub beef tenderloin with olive oil and season with salt and pepper. Place on rack in a shallow roasting pan. Roast until internal temperature of 135°F for medium-rare and 145°F for medium (temperature preferred by most class students), about 35 to 45 minutes. Remove tenderloin from roasting pan; cover with foil while finishing sauce.

For sauce: Melt 2 tablespoons butter in a large skillet over medium heat. Add leeks and garlic; cook stirring often until tender. Increase heat to high; add mushrooms and cook until mushrooms begin to brown. Add Marsala and stock; cook until liquid is reduced in half. (Note: Sauce may be made 1 day ahead to this point. For best flavor, strain mushrooms from sauce and refrigerate each separately.)

Place roasting pan over medium-high heat. Add mushroom sauce to drippings in pan; stir and heat until mushrooms are heated. Remove pan from heat; gradually whisk in chilled butter. Season with salt and pepper. Cut tenderloin into medallions and serve with sauce.

Makes 6 to 8 servings

Brown Sauce

Brown sauce is a rich sauce made of beef stock, onions, carrots, celery, herbs, and tomatoes. Use it as a stand-alone sauce or as an ingredient in other sauces served with beef. Make the sauce ahead and freeze portions of it to have ready for use anytime. It makes the best beef brisket!

Ingredients

6 tablespoons butter	6 tablespoons flour
1 cup chopped onion	2 tablespoons tomato paste
½ cup chopped carrot	4 cups (32 ounces) beef stock
½ cup chopped celery	1 small bay leaf

Melt butter in a large saucepan over medium-high heat until melted. Stir in onion, carrot, and celery; cook stirring often until vegetables are tender and beginning to brown. Stir in flour and cook until golden brown. Stir in tomato paste. Add stock and bay leaf; bring to a boil.

Reduce heat and simmer uncovered for 30 minutes. Strain the vegetables from the sauce, pressing to get all of the juices; discard vegetables.

Makes 2½ to 3 cups sauce

Demi-Glace

Demi-glace takes brown sauce one step further, cooking it with additional beef stock and sherry, Madeira, or red wine until it is reduced in half to a thick glaze that coats a spoon.

Ingredients

1½ to 3 cups Brown Sauce	2 tablespoons dry sherry, Madeira,
1½ cups (12 ounces) beef stock	or dry red wine

Combine all ingredients in a medium saucepan; simmer uncovered for 30 minutes or until reduced to a thick glaze that coats the back of a spoon.

Makes 1½ to 2¼ cups sauce

CAROL'S TIDBITS

Use Brown Sauce in Bourbon Sauce (page 109) and to make Beef Brisket (page 109). Use Demi-Glace in Irish Beef Tenders (page 108).

Sauces may be made ahead and refrigerated 3 days, or frozen for 6 months.

A typical demi-glace is made with equal amounts of brown sauce and stock. If the entire brown sauce recipe of 2½ to 3 cups is used, the demi-glace will have more depth with a less pronounced beef flavor.

Irish Beef Tenders

CAROL'S TIDBITS

Demi-glace is a rich brown sauce used as an ingredient in sauces. Look for it in the deli or meat department. It is easy to make and great to have on hand; see page 107 for recipe. A prepared gravy or sauce mix can also be doctored to be used as a substitute.

Skillets without nonstick surfaces develop more browned meat bits on the bottom of the pan which make sauces especially flavorful. These bits are sometimes called fond.

Here is a great St. Pat's Day alternative to corned beef and cabbage. For the richest, smoothest flavor, be sure to use a dark beer.

Ingredients

2 to 2½ pounds beef petite shoulder tender roasts
Olive oil, about 2 tablespoons
Coarse salt
Freshly ground black pepper
¾ cup (6 ounces) dark beer
1¼ cups (10 ounces) Demi-Glace (page 107)

½ cup (2 ounces) julienne strips of smoked ham
2 tablespoons minced shallot
1 clove garlic, minced
1 tablespoon chopped fresh parsley

Preheat oven to 425°F. Lightly brush roasts with olive oil and season with salt and pepper. Heat 1 tablespoon olive oil in a large skillet over high heat. Add roasts and sear on all sides until evenly browned. Place roasts on a rack in a shallow roasting pan; reserve drippings in skillet. Roast to internal temperature of 140° to 145°F for medium, about 15 to 20 minutes. Cover with foil and let stand for 10 minutes before slicing.

Slowly add beer to drippings in the skillet; heat until bubbles disappear. Add demi-glace, ham, shallot, and garlic; simmer until reduced to consistency of heavy cream. Add parsley and serve with sliced roasts.

Makes 6 to 8 servings

Bourbon Sauce

A delicious sauce served with any beef, from burgers to tenderloin, this sauce uses one of Kentucky's favorite homegrown ingredients.

Ingredients

1 tablespoon butter
3 tablespoons finely chopped shallot
1 clove garlic, minced
¼ cup bourbon
1 cup Brown Sauce (page 107)

¼ cup heavy whipping cream
1 teaspoon chopped fresh thyme
1 teaspoon chopped fresh rosemary
Coarse salt and freshly ground black pepper

Melt butter in a small saucepan over medium heat. Add shallot and garlic; cook stirring often until tender. Add bourbon and cook until bourbon is reduced in half. Stir in Brown Sauce and cook until thickened, about 5 minutes. Stir in heavy cream, thyme, and rosemary; cook until heated through. Season with salt and pepper.

Makes about 1 cup sauce

Excellent Beef Brisket

Beef brisket can serve many people and is a great family make-ahead. It requires long, slow cooking with added liquid to tenderize it. Brown Sauce is that perfect liquid addition. It adds flavor to the meat and the juices from cooking are ready to serve as sauce for mashed potatoes.

Brown brisket in a Dutch oven; then add ¼ cup Brown Sauce (page 107) for every pound of meat. Cover and bake at 325°F for 1 hour per pound meat.

This is a great recipe to prepare in a slow cooker.

Teriyaki Steak with Mushroom Sauce

CAROL'S TIDBITS

This steak is delicious with or without the sauce.

Internal temperature of meat increases about 5°F during standing. Steak cooked to medium will feel just firm to the touch.

The secret to tender meat is thinly slicing it almost parallel to the cutting board.

Teriyaki is a classic Japanese marinade of soy, sherry or sake, garlic, and ginger frequently used for chicken and beef. Grilling adds a caramelized glaze to the meat that makes it taste so wonderful with the fresh mushroom sauce.

Ingredients

1 beef flank, sirloin, or London Broil steak (1½ to 2 pounds)
½ cup dry sherry
¼ cup less sodium soy sauce
1 tablespoon brown sugar

1 tablespoon olive oil
2 cloves garlic, minced
1 teaspoon dried basil
½ teaspoon ground ginger

Mushroom Sauce
2 tablespoons butter
12 ounces baby bella mushrooms, sliced
2 tablespoons plus 1 teaspoon cornstarch

1 cup (8 ounces) beef stock
Coarse salt
Freshly ground black pepper
Chopped fresh parsley

Score surface of steak. Place in a large freezer-weight reclosable plastic bag. Combine sherry, soy sauce, brown sugar, olive oil, garlic, basil, and ginger; pour over steak. Seal bag and turn to coat meat. Place bag on plate and marinate meat in refrigerator for several hours or overnight.

Preheat grill to high. Remove steak from bag (reserve ½ cup marinade). Place on grill grid; cover and grill until internal temperature of 135°F for medium rare and 140° to 145°F for medium, about 4 to 6 minutes per side. Cover with foil and let stand for 10 minutes before slicing.

For the sauce: Melt butter in a large skillet over medium-high heat. Add sliced mushrooms and cook until tender. Stir cornstarch into reserved marinade until dissolved; stir marinade and stock into mushrooms. Cook stirring often until sauce is thickened and clear. Season with salt and pepper.

Slice steak thinly across the grain; serve with Mushroom Sauce and sprinkle with chopped parsley.

Makes 6 to 8 servings

Tuscan Grilled Flank Steak

A simple marinade of olive oil and fresh herbs adds robust flavor to grilled steak and red bell pepper. You will love the tangy Gorgonzola cheese crumbled over the juicy, thinly sliced beef.

Ingredients

1 beef flank, sirloin, or London Broil steak (1½ pounds)
1 large red bell pepper, quartered and seeded
¼ cup extra virgin olive oil

1 tablespoon chopped fresh rosemary
3 large cloves garlic, minced
Coarse salt
Freshly ground black pepper
Crumbled Gorgonzola cheese

Score surface of steak. Place steak and peppers in a large freezer-weight reclosable plastic bag. Combine olive oil, rosemary, and garlic; pour over steak and peppers. Seal bag and turn to coat. Place bag on a plate and marinate for at least 30 minutes and up to 12 hours.

Preheat grill to high. Remove steak and peppers from bag; discard marinade. Season steak with salt and pepper. Place on grill grid; cover and grill until browned and internal temperature of 145°F for medium, about 4 to 6 minutes per side. Cover with foil and let stand for 10 minutes before slicing.

Meanwhile, place peppers on grill grid or preheated grill pan; grill turning occasionally until crisp-tender and lightly charred, about 6 to 8 minutes. Cut into bite-size pieces.

Slice steak thinly across the grain; top with grilled peppers and Gorgonzola cheese.

Makes 6 servings

CAROL'S TIDBITS

London Broil is not a specific cut of meat but is usually top round, a lean economical cut of beef that benefits from marinating. Scoring the steak helps the marinade penetrate into the meat.

Italian Beef
In Red Wine

CAROL'S TIDBITS

If time permits, refrigerate cooked roast in the juices overnight. It will be easier to remove the fat and the meat will absorb more flavor.

If a thicker sauce is desired, dissolve 1 tablespoon cornstarch in 1 tablespoon water. Stir into juices and cook until thickened. Add sliced or shredded beef and heat.

Red wine blends are usually the best choice for cooking.

.

Slow, moist cooking is the secret to fall-apart beef. This beef is a perfect choice to prepare in a slow cooker to serve at your next tailgate party or on a cold winter night.

Ingredients

Olive oil
1 beef brisket or sirloin tip roast
　(3 to 5 pounds)
1 cup coarsely chopped onion
8 ounces sliced fresh mushrooms
2 cloves garlic, minced
1 teaspoon dried basil
1 teaspoon dried oregano
½ teaspoon dried thyme

½ teaspoon dried rosemary
½ teaspoon coarse salt
¼ teaspoon sugar
1 cup dry red wine
1 can (14.5 ounces) reduced
　sodium beef broth
¼ cup tomato paste with Italian
　herbs

Preheat oven to 325°F. Heat 1 tablespoon olive oil in a large skillet over high heat. Sear roast until browned on all sides adding additional oil if necessary. Place roast in a roasting pan; set aside.

Add onion, mushrooms, garlic, basil, oregano, thyme, rosemary, salt, and sugar to skillet; cook over medium-high heat stirring often until vegetables are tender. Spoon vegetables over roast. Deglaze the skillet with red wine. Stir in broth and tomato paste; bring to a boil. Pour over roast; cover and bake for 3 to 4 hours until meat is very tender.

Remove roast from pan juices; slice or shred meat. Skim fat from surface of juices; return meat to sauce. Serve meat on sliced buns, over noodles, or with mashed potatoes.

Makes 8 to 12 servings

Layered Enchilada Casserole

I'm frequently asked what my family likes to eat. This is it! "Mexican Casserole" was first developed for a microwave class when our sons were very young and it became a favorite. It is still at the top of Mike's request list.

Ingredients

2 pounds lean ground beef
1 tablespoon chili powder
1 to 1½ teaspoons ground cumin
½ teaspoon garlic powder
¼ teaspoon seasoned salt
1 can (10 ¾ ounces) cream of chicken soup
1 can (10 ¾ ounces) cream of mushroom soup

2 cans (10 ounces each) mild enchilada sauce
12 (6 or 7-inch) flour tortillas, cut into 1-inch wide strips
12 ounces (3 cups) shredded Mexican cheese blend

Preheat oven to 350°F. Crumble ground beef into a large microwave-safe casserole dish; microwave on high for 5 minutes. Drain meat; stir in chili powder, cumin, garlic powder, and seasoned salt; microwave 2 additional minutes. Stir in chicken soup, mushroom soup, and enchilada sauce. Cover casserole with lid or wax paper; microwave on high for 5 minutes stirring once.

Spread a thin layer of the meat sauce over bottom of a 9x13-inch baking dish coated with no-stick cooking spray. Top with half of the tortilla strips, half of the remaining sauce, and half of the cheese; repeat layers with remaining sauce, tortilla strips, and cheese.

Cover with foil and bake for 45 minutes or until edges are bubbly and center is hot. Remove foil and bake until cheese is lightly browned, about 5 to 10 additional minutes. Let stand for 10 minutes before serving.

Makes 8 to 10 servings

CAROL'S TIDBITS

Chopped onion is optional to cook with the meat. One cup sliced ripe olives and a small can of chopped green chiles are also optional additions with the enchilada sauce.

Can sizes for enchilada sauce vary depending on stores and regions of the country. If necessary to use part of an additional can of sauce, just freeze the remainder for the next time you make the casserole. Hot enchilada sauce can be used if you like spicy hot food.

Lower fat tortillas are preferred; soft tortillas get mushy.

Burgers Grande

For food safety, burgers should be cooked until well done (165 °F).

Ground chuck is 80% to 85% lean.

Ground round is 85% to 90% lean.

Ground sirloin is 90% to 92% lean.

Ground beef is a combination of cuts with % lean indicated on the label.

For a change of pace, grill these Tex-Mex burgers at your next barbecue. Serve with margaritas, tortilla chips, and fresh fruit.

Ingredients

1 loaf ciabatta bread
3 tablespoons butter, softened
1 teaspoon chili powder
1 clove garlic, minced
2½ pounds lean ground beef
½ cup chopped onion
½ cup salsa

1 tablespoon chili powder
1½ teaspoons oregano
1 teaspoon ground cumin
1 teaspoon coarse salt
Thinly sliced tomatoes
Sliced, pitted ripe olives

Guacamole

2 large ripe avocados, pitted and peeled
1 tablespoon fresh lime juice
1 small tomato, peeled, seeded, and finely chopped

2 tablespoons finely chopped onion
½ teaspoon coarse salt
Hot pepper sauce

Slice ciabatta bread in half horizontally. Combine butter, chili powder, and garlic in a small bowl. Spread over cut surfaces of bread; set aside.

Preheat grill to high. Combine ground beef, onion, salsa, chili powder, oregano, cumin, and salt in a mixing bowl; mix well. Shape into 8 flat patties. Place patties on grill grid; grill until browned and cooked in the center, about 4 to 5 minutes on each side. Place bread halves on grid and grill until lightly toasted, about 4 to 5 minutes.

Cut each ciabatta half into 8 squares. Slide burgers onto bottom squares and top with tomatoes, guacamole, olives, and ciabatta tops.

For guacamole: Combine avocados and lime juice in a mixing bowl; mash with a fork. Blend in tomato, onion, salt, and hot pepper sauce.

Makes 8 burgers

Sherried Chicken Breasts

This has been a longtime favorite of our son, Matt. The chicken breasts bake in an Alfredo sauce that he loves on noodles or fettuccine.

Ingredients

6 boneless, skinless chicken breast halves (2½ to 3 pounds)
Coarse salt
Freshly ground black pepper
½ cup dry sherry
2 tablespoons fresh lemon juice

3 tablespoons butter
3 tablespoons all-purpose flour
Half-and-half
Salt and pepper
Grated Parmesan cheese

Preheat oven to 400°F. Place chicken breasts in a shallow 2-quart baking dish coated with no-stick cooking spray. Season with salt and pepper. Combine sherry and lemon juice; pour over chicken. Loosely cover baking dish with foil; bake for 30 minutes. Pour liquid from baking dish into a 2-cup liquid measure; reserve. Cover chicken with foil while preparing sauce.

Melt butter in a medium saucepan; whisk in flour and cook until bubbly. Combine reserved liquid with enough cream to measure 1½ cups liquid. Stir liquid into flour mixture; cook over medium heat stirring often until smooth and thickened. Season with salt and pepper. Pour over chicken; sprinkle with Parmesan. Return chicken to oven; bake uncovered for 10 to 15 minutes or until bubbly. For a more golden appearance, heat under broiler at end of baking time.

Makes 6 servings

CAROL'S TIDBITS

To make ahead, it is best to chill baked chicken after pouring off liquid and cool sauce before pouring over chicken and refrigerating. To reheat, bake chicken at 350°F for 30 to 45 minutes.

Pan-Seared Breast of Chicken with Wild Mushroom & Sherry Sauce

CAROL'S TIDBITS

Wild mushrooms refer to mushrooms other than the common white button variety. Most any edible mushroom can be used in this recipe; the flavor will differ depending on the mushrooms.

Remove gills from large portabella mushrooms or the sauce will be muddy in appearance.

Dried mushrooms need to be reconstituted before using.

If desired, quickly brown chicken over high heat and finish cooking in a 375°F oven. Bake chicken 15 minutes.

Mushroom lovers take note. This rich and delicious recipe is for you! Use chanterelle mushrooms when available instead of baby bellas. Prepare ingredients ahead for quick, last minute cooking.

Ingredients

6 boneless, skinless chicken breast halves (2½ to 3 pounds)
Olive oil for brushing
Coarse salt
Freshly ground black pepper
2 tablespoons butter
¼ cup finely chopped onion

1 clove garlic, minced
12 ounces mixed baby bella and stemmed shiitake mushrooms
1 teaspoon minced fresh marjoram
½ cup dry sherry
1 cup (8 ounces) heavy whipping cream

Flatten chicken breasts just until uniform thickness. Brush with olive oil and season with salt and pepper. Heat a large skillet over medium-high heat. Add chicken and cook until outside is golden and juices run clear when pierced in center (165°F), about 6 minutes per side. Transfer chicken to a large plate and cover with foil to keep warm while preparing sauce.

Add butter, onion, and garlic to the skillet; cook over medium-high heat until onion is tender. Cut mushrooms into quarters. Stir mushrooms and marjoram into onion; cook until tender, about 5 minutes. Season with salt and pepper. Transfer mushrooms to plate with chicken; cover.

Add sherry to the skillet; stir over medium heat to scrape up any browned bits in bottom of pan. Add cream and cook until reduced and thickened. Season with salt and pepper.

Thinly slice chicken and fan out slices on serving plate. Top with mushrooms and sauce.

Makes 6 servings

Chicken and Prosciutto Spiedini

This is one of my favorite recipes for summer entertaining. The spiedini can be shaped ahead of time for minimal time in the kitchen after guests arrive. Delegate the grilling to someone else and entertaining will be a breeze.

Ingredients

6 boneless, skinless chicken breast halves (6 to 8 ounces each)
1 cup unseasoned dry bread crumbs
½ cup grated Parmesan cheese
¾ teaspoon dried basil
¾ teaspoon dried oregano
¾ teaspoon garlic powder

½ teaspoon salt
3 tablespoons butter, melted
3 tablespoons extra virgin olive oil
12 thin slices prosciutto ham
6-inch wooden skewers, soaked in water for 30 minutes

Butterfly chicken breasts and place each between 2 sheets of plastic wrap; pound chicken with a mallet until ¼-inch thickness.

Combine bread crumbs, Parmesan, basil, oregano, garlic powder, and salt in a shallow plate. Combine butter and olive oil in another shallow plate. Dip chicken in butter mixture and then coat with crumb mixture. Reserve any remaining crumb mixture. Place each chicken breast on a sheet of plastic wrap; top with 2 slices prosciutto. Fold in sides to enclose prosciutto and roll up chicken. Wrap each roll tightly in plastic wrap, twisting ends to secure; it will look like a sausage. Chill at least 1 hour.

Slice each roll into 1-inch-thick pinwheels, about 4 slices per roll. Thread slices onto skewers, about 3 slices per skewer. Sprinkle any remaining crumb mixture over chicken. Skewers can be refrigerated for several hours or grilled immediately.

Preheat grill to medium-high. Place skewers on lightly oiled grill grid; cover and grill 4 to 6 minutes per side until internal temperature of 165°F and chicken is golden brown.

Makes 6 to 8 servings

CAROL'S TIDBITS

Tips for flattening chicken: Remove tenderloin from chicken breast; set aside. Use a long, sharp knife to butterfly breast starting at the thinnest long side and cutting almost to the thickest side. Place opened breast on a sheet of plastic wrap with tenderloin down the center. Cover chicken with plastic wrap. Working from the center to the outside, lightly pound with edge of mallet to soften chicken before using the flat side of mallet to flatten it to ¼-inch thickness.

Make extra spiedini and freeze up to 2 months; thaw in refrigerator before grilling.

I like to serve the spiedini with risotto and grilled asparagus or zucchini.

Asian Grilled Chicken Tenders

CAROL'S TIDBITS

This marinade can also be used on chicken breasts, flattened to uniform thickness. Grill about 5 minutes per side or until chicken tests done.

Flat skewers work best to keep the tenders from twirling when turned on the grill.

Skewers are optional, but it is the traditional Indonesian way to serve grilled chicken with a peanut butter and soy sauce marinade. The tenders may be served as an entrée or fun appetizer.

Ingredients

1½ pounds chicken tenders
½ cup less sodium soy sauce
¼ cup creamy peanut butter
1 tablespoon dark sesame oil
1 tablespoon rice vinegar
1 clove garlic, minced
1½ teaspoons sugar

½ teaspoon crushed red pepper flakes
½ teaspoon grated fresh ginger
Wooden skewers, soaked in water for 30 minutes
2 tablespoons sesame seed, toasted

Place chicken tenders in a large freezer-weight reclosable plastic bag. Combine soy sauce, peanut butter, sesame oil, rice vinegar, garlic, sugar, pepper flakes, and ginger; blend until a smooth consistency and pour over chicken. Marinate chicken in refrigerator up to 3 hours.

Preheat grill to medium-high. Thread chicken tenders on skewers; sprinkle with sesame seed. Discard marinade. Place skewers on oiled grill grid. Cover and grill until golden brown, about 3 to 4 minutes per side.

Makes 4 to 6 servings

Grilled Jamaican Jerk Turkey Tenderloin

Jerk is a popular blend of seasonings used in Jamaican cooking that lends a sweet heat to many foods, especially poultry and pork. The jerk spices used on this turkey tenderloin are not fiery hot but are a wonderful complement to the mango fruit salsa.

Ingredients

2 tablespoons onion powder
1 tablespoon brown sugar
1 tablespoon coarse ground black pepper
2 teaspoons ground allspice
1½ teaspoons dried thyme

1 teaspoon coarse salt
½ teaspoon cayenne pepper
½ teaspoon ground cinnamon
½ teaspoon freshly grated nutmeg
2 turkey tenderloins (1½ pounds each)
Vegetable oil

Mango Salsa

1½ cups diced mango
2 tablespoons chopped red onion
1 tablespoon fresh lime juice

1 tablespoon chopped fresh mint, cilantro, or Italian parsley

Combine onion powder, brown sugar, black pepper, allspice, thyme, salt, cayenne pepper, cinnamon, and nutmeg in a small bowl. Rub turkey tenderloins with vegetable oil and then with the spice mixture; set aside.

For salsa: Combine mango, onion, and lime juice in a small bowl; refrigerate. Stir in mint just before serving.

Preheat grill to high heat. Place tenderloins on grill grid and reduce heat to medium; grill about 10 minutes per side until internal temperature of 165˚F. Let tenderloins rest 5 minutes before slicing across grain into thin slices. Serve with Mango Salsa.

Makes 6 servings

CAROL'S TIDBITS

Increase the amount of pepper, especially cayenne if you like hot and spicy food.

Fresh pineapple, papaya, peaches, nectarines, or a combination of fruits may be used in the salsa as well as mangoes.

Roast Turkey Tenderloins with Sweet Potato and Apple Hash

CAROL'S TIDBITS

To know when sauces are reduced in half, put half of the liquid to be reduced into the saucepan; stand the handle of a wooden spoon in the liquid to measure the height of the liquid. Tie dental floss or kitchen string on the line where the liquid begins; add the remainder of the liquid to the pan. As the liquid simmers, insert the spoon handle to check on the progress of the reduction. The liquid is reduced when it is at the line marked on the handle.

Granny Smith apples are a tart contrast to mild sweet potatoes. Both are enhanced by the hazelnut liqueur. Stir the sweet potatoes and apples occasionally as they roast to cook more uniformly.

Frangelico is a hazelnut liqueur.

An alternative to roasting a whole turkey is roasting turkey tenderloins with sweet potatoes and apples. The Marsala sauce adds a sweet, smoky flavor.

Ingredients

Marsala Sauce

1 cup dry Marsala wine
2 tablespoons chopped shallot
1 large clove garlic, minced
4 cups (32 ounces) reduced sodium
   chicken broth

2 tablespoons Marsala wine or water
2 tablespoons cornstarch
½ teaspoon chopped fresh thyme
Coarse salt and pepper
2 tablespoons cold butter, cubed

Sweet Potato and Apple Hash

2 teaspoons olive oil
6 slices bacon, diced
1 cup chopped onion
1 cup (8 ounces) reduced sodium
   chicken broth

¼ cup Frangelico or apple juice
4 cups cubed peeled sweet potatoes
2 cups cubed Granny Smith apples
1 teaspoon chopped fresh thyme
1 teaspoon chopped fresh rosemary

Turkey Tenderloins

2 turkey tenderloins (1½ pounds each)
Olive oil

Chopped fresh thyme and rosemary
Coarse salt and pepper

For sauce: Combine 1 cup Marsala, shallot, and garlic in a large saucepan; boil over medium heat until reduced by half, about 5 minutes. Add the 4 cups broth; boil until reduced by half, about 20 minutes. Set aside. (Recipe can be made the day before to this point).

For hash: In a large skillet, heat olive oil over medium heat. Stir in bacon and sauté until beginning to brown. Stir in onion and cook until tender. Stir in the 1 cup broth and liqueur; bring to a boil. Stir in sweet potatoes, apples, thyme, and rosemary. Set aside.

For turkey: Preheat oven to 400°F. Place turkey tenderloins in a shallow roasting pan that has been coated with no-stick cooking spray. Brush with olive oil and season with fresh herbs, salt, and pepper. Roast for 15 minutes. Spoon hash mixture around turkey and continue roasting until internal temperature of 165°F and vegetables are tender, about 25 to 30 additional minutes. Remove turkey and hash from roasting pan; cover with foil while finishing sauce.

Place roasting pan over medium-high heat and deglaze with Marsala mixture. Combine the 2 tablespoons Marsala, cornstarch, and thyme; stir into broth and cook until mixture thickens. Season with salt and pepper. Remove pan from heat and whisk in butter.

Makes 6 to 8 servings

Herb-Roasted Turkey Breast

Herb butter rubbed under and on the skin of turkey adds so much flavor you will always do this in the future. Cooking the turkey on a bed of vegetables keeps the meat very moist and makes a very flavorful broth for gravy.

Ingredients

1 turkey breast (6 to 7 pounds)
4 tablespoons butter, softened
1 clove garlic, minced
1 teaspoon dried or 1 tablespoon
  fresh thyme leaves
1 teaspoon rubbed sage
½ teaspoon coarse salt

¼ teaspoon cayenne pepper
Fresh sage leaves
1 cup coarsely chopped onion
1 cup coarsely chopped celery
1 cup coarsely chopped carrot
1 cup (8 ounces) chicken broth

Pat dry turkey with paper towels. Blend butter, garlic, thyme, rubbed sage, salt, and cayenne pepper. Slide hand under skin of turkey breast to loosen skin. Rub about half of the butter mixture over breast under skin. Arrange several sage leaves under skin.

Preheat oven to 350°F. Spread chopped onion, celery, and carrot in a shallow roasting pan. Pour broth over vegetables and place turkey breast on vegetables. Melt remaining butter mixture and brush over entire turkey breast. Roast turkey until internal temperature of 165°F, about 2½ to 3 hours. Cover turkey with foil during roasting if skin is becoming too brown. Tent roasted turkey with foil and let stand 10 minutes before slicing.

Note: Generally plan to roast a turkey breast for 22 to 25 minutes per pound. Refer to the roasting directions which come with the turkey breast for the time recommended for that particular turkey. Whole, unstuffed turkeys roast in slightly less time per pound of meat.

CAROL'S TIDBITS

Use this method for roasting whole turkeys. Also put vegetables and sprigs of fresh herbs inside the cavity.

Serve turkey with Sausage Mushroom Dressing (page 147).

Sandwiches have been a favorite use for leftover turkey, but Turkey Wild Rice Soup (page 74) might become the new favorite.

Lime Teriyaki Grilled Salmon

CAROL'S TIDBITS

I prefer the wider head end portion of a salmon fillet. The greater thickness allows the salmon to get a crispy surface with a moist interior. The tail end has good flavor but is difficult to grill without overcooking.

The glaze is added after the flesh-side is browned and turned to prevent the honey and soy from burning. The foil catches any drips for easy clean-up.

.

One word describes this grilled salmon...Awesome! It scores big flavor points and you will love the grilling method.

Ingredients

½ cup less sodium soy sauce
¼ cup dry sherry
2 teaspoons cornstarch
⅓ cup honey
1 tablespoon grated fresh ginger
1 teaspoon grated lime peel

1 tablespoon fresh lime juice
2 tablespoons vegetable oil
2 pounds salmon fillet, cut into
  6 pieces
Black and red pepper blend

Combine soy sauce, sherry, and cornstarch in a small saucepan; stir until cornstarch is dissolved. Cook over medium-high heat, stirring often, until sauce thickens. Remove from heat; stir in honey, ginger, lime peel and juice. Remove ¼ cup sauce for basting salmon; reserve remaining sauce to serve with grilled salmon.

Preheat grill to medium-high. Brush vegetable oil over salmon and sprinkle with pepper blend. Place salmon, flesh-side down, on oiled grill grid; cover and grill for 4 minutes. Place sheet of foil on grid; turn salmon skin-side down on top of foil. Brush basting sauce over salmon. Cover and grill until opaque throughout and internal temperature of 145˚F, about 4 to 5 minutes. Slide metal spatula between flesh and skin. Skin will stick to foil; discard foil. Serve salmon with reserved sauce.

Makes 6 servings

Grilled Salmon With Thai Cucumber Relish

A Thai-rific grilled salmon with a light refreshing cucumber salsa! The salsa is also good with chicken, such as Asian Grilled Chicken Tenders on page 118.

on page 118.

Ingredients

Thai Cucumber Relish

2 medium cucumbers, peeled, seeded, and diced (2½ to 3 cups)
¼ cup chopped red onion
½ teaspoon coarse salt

¼ cup rice wine vinegar
¼ cup sugar
1½ teaspoons grated fresh ginger
1 tablespoon chopped cilantro

Salmon

2 pounds salmon fillet, cut into 6 pieces
¼ cup less sodium soy sauce
2 tablespoons vegetable oil

1 tablespoon brown sugar
½ teaspoon crushed red pepper flakes
1 clove garlic, minced
Freshly ground black pepper

For relish: Combine cucumbers, onion, and salt in a medium bowl; let stand for at least 15 minutes. Combine vinegar and sugar in a glass measure; microwave on high for 1 minute. Stir to dissolve sugar; cool to lukewarm or cooler. Drain off any liquid from cucumbers. Stir ginger into vinegar and combine with cucumbers. Refrigerate until serving time. Stir in cilantro just before serving.

Place salmon in a shallow dish. Combine soy sauce, vegetable oil, brown sugar, pepper flakes, and garlic; pour over salmon and marinate while grill preheats to medium-high.

Place salmon, flesh-side down, on oiled grill grid; cover and grill for 4 minutes. Place sheet of foil on grid; turn salmon skin-side down on foil. Cover and grill until opaque throughout and internal temperature is 145˚F, about 4 to 5 minutes. Slide metal spatula between flesh and skin. Skin will stick to foil; discard foil.

Sprinkle salmon with pepper and serve with Thai Cucumber Relish.

Makes 6 servings

CAROL'S TIDBITS

If you prefer salmon steaks, grill 1-inch-thick steaks for 4 to 5 minutes per side; omit the foil. The general rule for grilling fish is 8 to 9 minutes per inch thickness.

Farm-raised salmon is usually milder in flavor and higher in fat than wild salmon. Most wild salmon comes from Alaska.

Creamy Dilled Shrimp Salad

CAROL'S TIDBITS

This salad would make delicious smørrebrød or Danish open-faced sandwiches. Smørrebrød (SMURH-uh-bruth) translates as "butter and bread" and is usually dense, dark rye bread topped with a wide variety of meats, cheese, seafood, eggs, and vegetables.

.

Sour cream dressing with cucumber, dill, and caraway give this shrimp salad a Scandinavian flair. Serve it on lettuce for a salad, with wooden picks for an appetizer, or on rye bread for an open-faced sandwich.

Ingredients

½ cup dairy sour cream
½ cup mayonnaise
½ cup peeled, seeded, and
   chopped cucumber
½ cup chopped red onion
1½ tablespoons chopped fresh dill
1½ teaspoons fresh lemon juice

1 clove garlic, minced
¼ teaspoon coarse salt
¼ teaspoon caraway seed
Freshly ground black pepper
8 drops hot pepper sauce
2 pounds peeled, deveined, and
   cooked shrimp

Combine all ingredients, except shrimp, in a large mixing bowl. Stir in shrimp. Chill until ready to serve. Serve on a bed of Bibb lettuce.

Makes 6 to 8 servings

VEGETABLES & SIDES

Meant to accompany your dinner entrée,
these vegetables and side dishes are so delicious
they may just upstage the main course!

Curried Butternut Squash with Apples and Sausage

This hearty vegetable casserole can be served as an entrée for brunch or dinner. I like to serve it with poultry dishes, especially **Pan-Seared Breast of Chicken with Wild Mushrooms and Sherry Sauce (page 116)**.

Ingredients

1 medium to large butternut squash, about 2 pounds	¾ teaspoon salt
4 ounces crumbled Italian sausage	¾ teaspoon curry powder
1 cup diced onion	¼ teaspoon jerk seasoning
1 red apple, cut into cubes	¼ teaspoon celery salt
¼ cup diced celery	¼ teaspoon dried rosemary, crushed
¼ cup diced green bell pepper	¼ teaspoon dried basil
2 tablespoons butter	⅛ teaspoon ground white pepper
	¼ to ½ cup grated Parmesan cheese

Microwave whole squash on high for 2 minutes. Cut in half, peel, and cut into ¾-inch cubes. Steam squash in a small amount of lightly salted water in a large saucepan over medium-high heat just until tender. Drain well; set aside.

Preheat oven to 350°F. Coat a shallow 2-quart baking dish with no-stick cooking spray; set aside. Cook sausage and onion in a large skillet over high heat stirring often just until sausage is no longer pink; blot with paper towels to remove any grease. Stir in all remaining ingredients, except squash and Parmesan; cook until sausage and onions are lightly browned. Stir in squash and turn mixture into baking dish; sprinkle with Parmesan. Bake 20 to 30 minutes, or until heated through.

Makes 6 to 8 servings

CAROL'S TIDBITS

This casserole may be prepared the day before and refrigerated. Increase baking time 10 to 15 additional minutes.

Each herb and spice adds a special flavor. If one or two are not in your pantry, the dish will still be delicious.

Choose butternut squash with a large neck and small rounded end.

Garlic and Lemon Grilled Asparagus

Asparagus can be served as a side dish or chilled for a salad. Enjoy garlic and zesty lemon on this grilled asparagus.

Ingredients

¼ cup extra virgin olive oil
2 cloves garlic, minced
2 pounds asparagus spears
2 teaspoons grated lemon peel

2 tablespoons fresh squeezed
   lemon juice
Coarse salt
Freshly ground black pepper

Combine olive oil and garlic in a small bowl; set aside for at least 30 minutes to infuse garlic flavor into oil. Trim tough ends from asparagus; rinse well and pat dry. Place asparagus in a shallow serving dish; drizzle garlic oil over asparagus. Grill asparagus immediately or let stand up to 1 hour.

Preheat grill to medium-high. Remove asparagus from garlic oil (reserve oil) and place diagonally on grill grid. Close grill cover and grill until spears begin to brown on bottom, about 2 to 4 minutes. Turn spears and continue to grill 2 to 3 additional minutes. Stir lemon juice into reserved garlic oil. Return asparagus to serving dish and spoon oil over spears; sprinkle with salt, pepper, and lemon peel.

Makes 6 servings

To roast asparagus: Preheat oven to 425°F. Line a shallow baking pan with foil. Arrange trimmed asparagus in a single layer on prepared pan. Brush with olive oil and roast turning once until crisp-tender and beginning to brown, about 10 minutes. Season with salt and pepper.

Hollandaise Sauce

Never fear making hollandaise sauce if you use this quick and easy recipe from one of my early microwave classes. I am told by many that this is the only hollandaise they will ever make. Serve it on steamed vegetables and eggs Benedict.

Ingredients

8 tablespoons (1 stick) butter
½ cup heavy whipping cream
4 egg yolks

3 tablespoons fresh lemon juice
½ teaspoon dry mustard
¼ teaspoon salt

Microwave butter in a 2-cup glass measure on high until melted, about 45 seconds. Combine remaining ingredients in a bowl; whisk until well blended. Stir egg mixture into melted butter. Microwave uncovered on high stirring every 30 seconds until thickened, about 1½ to 2½ minutes.

Makes 1¼ cups sauce

CAROL'S TIDBITS

One teaspoon Dijon mustard may be substituted for dry mustard.

I often serve hollandaise as a dipping sauce for steamed artichokes; our sons called it artichoke gravy.

Spinach-Basil Sauce

Serve this creamy pesto sauce on green beans, sliced tomatoes, as a dip for crudités, and as a sandwich spread. There are many possibilities; you will love it.

Ingredients

1 cup packed spinach leaves
⅓ cup packed basil leaves
¼ cup grated Parmesan cheese
1 clove garlic, minced

½ cup mayonnaise
½ cup Greek yogurt or dairy sour
  cream
Salt and pepper

Place spinach, basil, Parmesan, and garlic in a food processor work bowl; process until leaves are finely minced. Add yogurt and mayonnaise; process until blended. Season with salt and pepper. Chill until ready to serve.

Makes 1½ cups sauce

CAROL'S TIDBITS

Reduced-fat yogurt and mayonnaise may be used in this flavor-packed sauce.

Sautéed Spinach
with Caramelized Onions

Sautéed spinach is fast, delicious, and very nutritious. No wonder Popeye loved it and he probably did not have the caramelized onions to make it extra delicious.

Ingredients

1 tablespoon olive oil
1 tablespoon butter
1 cup slivered onion
½ teaspoon sugar

1 clove garlic, thinly slivered
10 ounces fresh spinach, rinsed
Coarse salt

Heat olive oil and butter in a Dutch oven over medium heat until oil bubbles. Add onion and sprinkle with sugar; cook stirring frequently until onions are golden brown. Remove onion with a slotted spoon; set aside.

Add garlic and spinach to Dutch oven; toss over medium-high heat just until spinach is wilted. Serve spinach topped with caramelized onion.

Makes 4 to 6 servings

Sautéed Summer Squash and Grape Tomatoes with Basil Butter

A basil-shallot butter can be made ahead to quickly season this stir-fry mixture of zucchini and yellow summer squash. Grape tomatoes added the last few minutes of cooking become very juicy and almost pop in your mouth.

Ingredients

1 medium zucchini (about 8 ounces)
1 medium yellow
  summer squash (about 8 ounces)
3 tablespoons Basil Butter

1 cup grape or cherry tomatoes
Coarse salt
Freshly ground black pepper

Basil Butter

8 tablespoons (1 stick) butter,
  softened
3 tablespoons chopped fresh or
  1 tablespoon dried basil

2 tablespoons minced shallot
1 clove garlic, minced
1 teaspoon lemon juice

Cut zucchini and squash into ¼x2-inch julienne strips or ¾-inch cubes; set aside.

Combine all ingredients for Basil Butter in a medium bowl; blend well. Melt 3 tablespoons of the butter in a large skillet over medium-high heat. Add zucchini and squash; cook stirring frequently until crisp-tender, about 5 minutes. Stir in tomatoes and cook just until tomatoes are warm. Remove from heat; season with salt and pepper.

Makes 6 servings

Green Beans with Toasted Garlic Butter Crumbs

CAROL'S TIDBITS

I use Pepperidge Farm bread or French baguettes to make crumbs.

Browned crumbs will become crisp after the beans are removed from skillet.

Also fun to make with yellow wax beans or use a combo of beans.

These beans have the best tasting, crispy, buttery crumbs; there are never any left behind in the serving bowl. Cook the beans ahead and toss with the crumbs just before serving. It isn't any easier than that.

Ingredients

1 pound fresh green beans, rinsed and stems removed

2 slices coarse textured bread

3 tablespoons butter

2 cloves garlic, minced

Coarse salt

Bring about 6 cups lightly salted water to a boil in a large saucepan over high heat. Add beans and cook 5 minutes; drain and rinse with cold water. Drain well; set aside.

Remove thick crusts from bread. Place bread in a food processor work bowl; process into coarse crumbs.

Melt butter in a large skillet over medium heat; add garlic and cook stirring often until garlic is just beginning to brown. Add beans and crumbs; increase heat to medium-high and stir until crumbs have browned, about 3 minutes. Season with salt.

Makes 6 servings

Broccoli with Ginger-Sesame Butter

Broccoli gets an Asian flavor from browned butter with toasted sesame seeds and fresh ginger.

Ingredients

1 medium bunch broccoli (about 1 pound)

4 tablespoons butter

2 tablespoons sesame seeds

1 teaspoon minced fresh ginger

Coarse salt

Cut broccoli into spears or bite-size florets. Place broccoli in a steamer basket over boiling water. Cover saucepan and steam until bright green and tender when pierced with a knife tip; about 5 to 7 minutes; drain.

Meanwhile, melt butter in a small skillet over medium heat; add sesame seeds and cook until seeds are toasted and butter is lightly browned. Remove from heat; stir in minced ginger and season with salt. Drizzle over broccoli.

Makes 4 servings

CAROL'S TIDBITS

Serve the seasoned butter on other vegetables like asparagus and green beans.

Look for fresh ginger, or gingerroot, in the the Asian produce section. It is a knobby root but should have a smooth skin which is easily peeled with the side of a teaspoon.

Brussels Sprouts with Carrots and Rosemary

CAROL'S TIDBITS

People love or hate Brussels sprouts. They have a very mild, delicate flavor when fresh but can get very strong if stored too long. Do not store longer than 3 days before cooking.

Best time of year to serve Brussels sprouts is August thru March. They are high in vitamins A and C.

Brussels sprouts resemble tiny cabbages making this an ideal recipe for St. Patrick's Day. I think it is also perfect for Thanksgiving or with a roast and mashed potatoes. Not a Brussels sprouts fan? Substitute broccoli.

Ingredients

4 tablespoons butter
⅓ cup thinly sliced onion
1 pound Brussels sprouts, trimmed and halved
1 pound peeled baby carrots

⅔ cup chicken broth
¾ teaspoon dried rosemary leaves
2 teaspoons sugar
Coarse salt
Freshly ground black pepper

Melt butter in a large skillet over medium heat. Add onion and cook until softened, about 2 minutes. Stir in Brussels sprouts, carrots, chicken broth, and rosemary. Cover and cook stirring occasionally until vegetables are tender, about 8 to 10 minutes. Stir in sugar and season with salt and pepper.

Makes 8 servings

Stir-Fry Vegetable Medley

This has been a long time favorite combination of vegetables to serve with most any entrée. The colorful vegetables can be prepared ahead for fast, last-minute cooking.

Ingredients

½ bunch broccoli (about 8 ounces)
3 large carrots, peeled (about 8 ounces)
1 medium zucchini (about 8 ounces)
4 ounces fresh mushrooms, quartered
2 tablespoons butter
1 clove garlic, minced

½ teaspoon coarse salt
½ teaspoon seasoned salt
¼ teaspoon sugar
⅛ teaspoon dried thyme
Dash cayenne pepper

Separate broccoli into bite-size florets and stems; set florets aside. Cut stems into thin slices and keep separate from florets. Cut carrots and zucchini into julienne sticks; combine with sliced stems.

Melt butter in a large skillet over medium-high heat; stir in garlic, coarse salt, seasoned salt, sugar, thyme, cayenne pepper, broccoli stems, carrots, and zucchini. Increase heat to high; stir-fry until vegetables begin to cook. Stir in broccoli florets and mushrooms; cover and continue to cook until vegetables are crisp tender, about 5 minutes.

Makes 4 to 6 servings

CAROL'S TIDBITS

Julienne sticks look like thin French fries.

Stir-fry more dense vegetables first and then add the more delicate vegetables to cook vegetables uniformly.

Lawry's is my favorite seasoned salt blend.

Honey-Bourbon Carrots

CAROL'S TIDBITS

Peeled and sliced carrots will have a more intense flavor than baby carrots. Baby carrots look more impressive for a special occasion, however.

Bourbon is a corn-based whiskey. Tennessee whiskey is also corn-based, but is filtered through sugar-maple charcoal giving it a sweeter flavor.

A spirited glaze adds a special touch to carrots making them especially tasty with roast beef and mashed potatoes.

Ingredients

1 pound carrots, peeled and sliced diagonally into ¼-inch thick slices
½ cup water
¼ cup honey

¼ cup bourbon whiskey
2 tablespoons butter
Coarse salt
Freshly ground black pepper

Combine all ingredients in a large skillet. Cover and cook over medium heat stirring occasionally for 5 to 10 minutes or until carrots are nearly tender. Remove cover and continue to cook stirring occasionally until carrots are tender and liquid is reduced to a glaze. Season with salt and pepper.

Makes 4 to 6 servings

Roasted Sweet Potatoes

CAROL'S TIDBITS

Vegetables brown best and are easier to stir if not roasted on foil or parchment. Spray baking pan well with no-stick cooking spray to aid clean-up.

Roasted sweet potatoes are easy to prepare and the bonus is that they are one of the most nutritious foods for us to eat.

Ingredients

2 pounds sweet potatoes, peeled and cut into 1-inch cubes
3 tablespoons olive oil, vegetable oil, or butter, melted

2 to 4 tablespoons brown sugar or pure maple syrup
Coarse salt

Preheat oven to 400°F. Coat a rimmed (preferably nonstick) baking sheet with no-stick cooking spray. Toss sweet potatoes with oil or butter; spread on prepared baking sheet. Bake 15 minutes; toss potatoes with brown sugar or maple syrup and season with salt. Bake 5 to 10 additional minutes or until potatoes are tender and lightly browned.

Makes 6 servings

Puréed
Sweet Potatoes

This is one of my favorite sweet potato recipes. The carrots add just enough complementing flavor to cut the monotony and sweetness of the potatoes alone. Be sure to try the Parmesan cheese and green onion additions.

Ingredients

1 pound carrots, peeled and sliced into ¾-inch-thick slices (2 to 2½ cups)

1½ pounds sweet potatoes, peeled and cut into 1-inch cubes (4 cups)

4 tablespoons butter, softened

½ teaspoon coarse salt

Freshly ground black pepper

Heavy whipping cream

Place carrots in a large saucepan and add enough water to cover. Cover and bring to a boil over high heat; reduce heat to medium-low and cook 10 minutes.

Add sweet potatoes and additional water if mostly absorbed by the carrots; cook 20 minutes or until sweet potatoes are very tender. Drain vegetables well and return to saucepan; stir over low heat until vegetables are dry.

Remove saucepan from heat and beat vegetables with an electric mixer until smooth. Add butter, salt, and pepper. Beat in enough cream to moisten vegetables.

Makes 6 to 8 servings

CAROL'S TIDBITS

Flavor Variations: Stir grated Parmesan cheese and sliced green onions into potato mixture with the butter, or sprinkle over potatoes when served.

Stir 2 tablespoons puréed chipotle chile peppers into potatoes before serving.

Puréed sweet potatoes make a great garnish when piped onto dinner plates.

Garlic
Mashed Potatoes

CAROL'S TIDBITS

Use a potato masher to mash potatoes for the fluffiest consistency. Potatoes will be gluey and sticky if mashed in a food processor or over-beaten with a mixer. A few lumps left in the potatoes are proof they were fresh cooked, not from a box.

For extra festive color and flavor, add 2 tablespoons chopped sun-dried tomatoes.

Celery root is an ugly, knobby root that adds awesome flavor to soups, stews, and these mashed potatoes! Celery root is a common name for celeriac, a special celery grown for its root. Its flavor is a cross between celery and parsley.

Roasted garlic and fresh basil make these mashed potatoes irresistible. They are great with roast chicken and beef, but I could be happy with a meal of just these.

Ingredients

3 pounds (about 4 large) Yukon gold potatoes, peeled and quartered

1 bulb garlic, roasted (page 13)

3 tablespoons finely shredded fresh basil

2 tablespoons butter, softened

2 tablespoons olive oil

¼ cup half-and-half, plus more as needed

2 tablespoons freshly grated Parmesan cheese

Coarse salt

Freshly ground black pepper

Place potatoes in a 3-quart saucepan; cover with cold water and season with salt. Bring water to a boil; reduce heat to a gentle boil and cook until potatoes are very tender, about 18 to 20 minutes.

Drain potatoes well and return to saucepan; stir over low heat until dry. Add roasted garlic, basil, butter, olive oil, and ¼ cup half-and-half. Mash potatoes with potato masher or mixer adding more half-and-half as necessary to reach desired consistency. Stir in Parmesan; season with salt and pepper.

Makes 6 to 8 servings

Celery Root Mashed Potatoes

Substitute 2 medium celery roots, peeled and cut into 1-inch cubes, for 1 pound of the potatoes. Cook celery root 5 minutes before adding potatoes and cooking according to above directions. Drain well and add 6 tablespoons softened butter.

Mash potatoes adding half-and-half or milk to moisten; season with salt, pepper, and freshly grated nutmeg.

138

Smashed Red Potatoes with Parmesan Basil Butter

Red creamer potatoes, also known as new potatoes, are very tender and creamy. Smashed potatoes taste like a cross between oven-roasted potatoes and mashed potatoes.

CAROL'S TIDBITS

Serve these potatoes in place of baked potatoes or mashed potatoes. They are especially good with beef entrées.

Ingredients

1 bag (24 ounces) red creamer potatoes
2 tablespoons olive oil
Coarse salt
Freshly ground black pepper
6 tablespoons butter, softened

3 tablespoons grated Parmesan cheese
3 cloves garlic, minced
¼ cup finely chopped fresh basil

Preheat oven to 375°F. Wash and dry potatoes; place in a large mixing bowl. Drizzle olive oil over potatoes and season with salt and pepper. Toss potatoes to coat with oil and seasonings. Place potatoes on a rimmed baking pan; set bowl aside. Bake until largest potatoes are tender when pierced with a fork, about 30 minutes.

Combine butter, Parmesan, garlic, and basil in the bowl; stir until blended. Add potatoes and smash with a potato masher or large spoon. Stir to blend potatoes into butter mixture. Season with salt and pepper.

Makes 4 to 6 servings

Rumbledethumps

CAROL'S TIDBITS

Can be made ahead and refrigerated; bring to room temperature before baking or increase baking time. Insert a knife in the center and gently touch it to your lips to determine if potatoes are heated through.

Flavor is significantly better when potatoes are cooked in the cabbage water versus plain water.

Serve on St. Patrick's Day with corned beef.

What are Rumbledethumps? It is an amazing Scottish potato, cabbage ,and cheese dish similar to Irish Colcannon or English Bubble & Squeak. It can be an entrée, but makes a delicious side dish for beef entrées. This recipe will become a favorite!

Ingredients

8 cups (28 ounces) thinly sliced green cabbage, 1 small to medium head
2½ to 3 pounds russet potatoes, peeled and cut into 2-inch pieces
8 tablespoons butter (1 stick), softened

¼ cup chopped chives
1 teaspoon coarse salt
Freshly ground black pepper
6 ounces (1½ cups) shredded sharp Cheddar cheese

Preheat oven to 350 °F. Coat a 3-quart shallow baking dish with no-stick cooking spray; set aside. Cook cabbage uncovered in a large saucepan of boiling salted water until tender, about 5 minutes. Transfer cabbage to a colander to drain (reserve cooking water).

Add potatoes to cooking water and cook until tender, about 10 to 15 minutes. Drain potatoes reserving a small amount of cooking water. Place potatoes in a large mixer bowl. Add butter and mash with a potato masher or mixer. Mix in chives, salt, and pepper. Stir in cabbage, adding a small amount of reserved cooking water if more moisture is desired.

Spoon potato mixture into baking dish; sprinkle cheese over the top. Bake 30 to 35 minutes or until heated through and cheese is melted.

Makes 10 to 12 servings

Planked Potatoes

Planked potatoes are really Duchess potatoes, but they are often called planked potatoes because they are piped on a tray or around food on a platter. Serve them with Swedish meatballs (page 34) for an entrée.

Ingredients

2 pounds Yukon gold or russet potatoes, peeled and cut into 3-inch pieces
4 tablespoons butter, melted and divided
¼ cup heavy whipping cream

2 egg yolks
1 teaspoon salt
½ teaspoon freshly grated nutmeg

Place potatoes in a 3-quart saucepan; cover with cold water and season with salt. Bring water to a boil; reduce heat to a gentle boil and cook until potatoes are very tender, about 18 to 20 minutes. Drain potatoes well; return to saucepan; stir over low heat until potatoes are dry.

Preheat oven to 425°F. Coat a foil-lined baking sheet with no-stick cooking spray. Mash potatoes with a potato masher or mixer, adding 2 tablespoons of the melted butter while mashing. Add cream, egg yolks, salt, and nutmeg; beat just until smooth and all ingredients are incorporated. Use a pastry bag fitted with a large star tip to pipe mounds of potatoes onto prepared baking sheet. (Potatoes may be refrigerated at this point to be baked later.)

Just before baking, brush potatoes with remaining melted butter. Bake until peaks of potatoes are nicely browned, about 15 to 20 minutes. For darker brown peaks, brown potatoes a few extra minutes under the broiler. (If potatoes are made ahead and refrigerated, increase baking time 5 to 10 additional minutes.)

Makes 6 to 8 servings

CAROL'S TIDBITS

Mashed potatoes need to be made with dry, mealy textured potatoes like russets. Red-skinned potatoes tend to be waxy and make gummy mashed potatoes. Yukon golds have a pleasant, buttery flavor. They are more mealy than red-skinned potatoes, but not as dry as russets.

Potatoes should not be cut too small when cooked or they will get water-logged and make runny mashed potatoes.

Spaghetti Squash
with Toasted Walnut Butter

CAROL'S TIDBITS

Blue cheese, Asiago, or feta cheese are great substitutes for Gorgonzola or Parmesan cheese.

For a quick supper, serve the squash with your favorite pasta sauce.

It is amazing how spaghetti can come from squash. The spaghetti-like strands are high in nutrients and fiber; low in calories and carbs. Use it in place of regular spaghetti in many recipes.

Ingredients

1 medium spaghetti squash (about 3 pounds)
4 tablespoons butter
½ cup coarsely chopped walnuts
1 clove garlic, minced

2 tablespoons chopped fresh parsley
½ teaspoon coarse salt
Freshly ground black pepper
Crumbled Gorgonzola or grated Parmesan cheese

Wash outside of the spaghetti squash and carefully make deep pierces into squash with tip of a sharp knife. Microwave squash on high for 5 minutes. Cut squash in half and place cut-side down in a microwave-safe baking dish. Microwave on high until fork-tender, allowing 5 to 6 minutes total cooking time per pound. Let stand for 10 to 15 minutes until cool enough to handle.

Cook walnuts and garlic in butter in a small skillet over low heat until butter begins to lightly brown.

Scoop out and discard seeds from center of squash. Scrape flesh using a fork to separate the spaghetti-like strands. Place in a large serving bowl. Toss squash with walnut butter and chopped parsley; season with salt and pepper. Serve with crumbled or grated cheese.

Makes 8 servings

Roasted Root Vegetables with Herb Butter

The peak season to serve roasted root vegetables is fall and winter shortly after they have been harvested. Rutabagas and parsnips may be unfamiliar vegetables, but this combination of carrots, leeks and herb butter will change that. I like to serve this with roast chicken and mashed potatoes.

Ingredients

2 large carrots, peeled
1 small rutabaga, peeled
3 to 4 small parsnips, peeled
1 leek, sliced

1 tablespoon olive oil
Coarse salt
Freshly ground black pepper

Herb Butter
4 tablespoons butter, softened
2 tablespoons finely chopped shallot
1 tablespoon chopped fresh or 1 teaspoon dried basil
1 tablespoon chopped fresh chives

1 large clove garlic, minced
1½ teaspoons fresh lemon juice
½ teaspoon fresh or ¼ teaspoon dried thyme
¼ teaspoon coarse salt

Preheat oven to 400°F. Line a 10x15x1-inch baking pan with foil; coat with no-stick cooking spray.

Cut carrots, rutabaga, and parsnips into julienne strips. Combine vegetables and olive oil on baking pan; toss to coat vegetables with oil. Roast 30 minutes.

Meanwhile, combine butter, shallot, basil, chives, garlic, lemon juice, thyme, and salt for herb butter in a small bowl; beat until well combined. Add half of the butter mixture to the partially roasted vegetables; toss to coat. Continue roasting vegetables until tender and lightly browned, about 15 to 20 minutes.

Toss with remaining herb butter; season with salt and pepper.

Makes 6 to 8 servings

CAROL'S TIDBITS

Julienne strips of vegetables will look like thin French fries.

Rutabagas are in the cabbage family and look like big turnips with waxed pale yellow and purple skin. Scandinavians call them Swedes and mix them into mashed potatoes.

Parsnips look like white carrots, but are firmer and less sweet.

Use only the white and pale green portion of leeks.

Garden Vegetable Couscous

CAROL'S TIDBITS

Couscous is a tiny pasta made with semolina, a coarse ground hard wheat flour. Its origin is North Africa.

Cooked chicken or shrimp are tasty protein additions.

Loaded with vegetables, this couscous is a vegetarian's delight. Serve with a salad for a simple meal or as a side with fish or chicken.

Ingredients

1½ cups (12 ounces) reduced sodium chicken or vegetable broth
1 cup couscous
2 tablespoons extra virgin olive oil
1½ cups cubed zucchini
1 cup slivered red onion
1½ cups (8 ounces) fresh or frozen corn

½ cup diced red bell pepper
½ teaspoon dried or 1½ teaspoons fresh thyme
½ teaspoon coarse salt
½ cup quartered pitted kalamata or ripe olives

Bring broth to a boil in a medium saucepan. Stir in couscous; remove from heat and let stand covered for 5 minutes.

Heat olive oil in a large skillet over medium-high heat. Add zucchini and onion; cook and stir until tender and lightly browned. Stir in corn, bell pepper, thyme and salt. Cook and stir until thoroughly heated. Remove from heat and stir in couscous and olives.

Makes 6 to 8 servings

144

Walnut Rice

Toasted walnuts and celery add flavor and texture to make ordinary rice just a bit more special. Serve this as a side to pork and poultry entrées.

Ingredients

2 tablespoons butter
½ cup diced celery
2 cloves garlic, minced and divided
1 cup long grain rice
2 cups (16 ounces) reduced-sodium
 chicken broth

¼ teaspoon coarse salt
Dash cayenne pepper
1 tablespoon walnut oil
½ cup coarsely chopped walnuts

Melt butter in a medium saucepan over medium-high heat. Stir in celery and half of the garlic; cook until celery is crisp-tender. Stir in rice; cook 3 to 4 minutes stirring frequently until rice begins to turn translucent. Add chicken broth, salt, and cayenne pepper; bring to a boil. Reduce heat; cover and simmer for 15 minutes.

Meanwhile, heat walnut oil in a small skillet. Add walnuts and remaining garlic; cook over medium heat stirring frequently until nuts begin to brown. Stir nuts into rice after rice has cooked 15 minutes. Season to taste. Let stand covered for 5 to 10 minutes. Fluff with a fork.

Makes 4 to 5 servings

CAROL'S TIDBITS

If softer rice is desired, add 2 to 4 tablespoons water after cooking 15 minutes; cook 5 additional minutes before adding nuts.

Rice is cooked in butter before adding broth to toast the rice and keep rice grains from getting gummy during cooking.

If walnut oil is not available, use extra virgin olive oil.

Wrap celery in foil to keep it fresh and crisp.

Roasted Vegetable Tortellini

CAROL'S TIDBITS

Vegetables can also be grilled on a grill pan over high heat; grill stirring occasionally until crisp-tender and lightly charred, about 6 to 8 minutes.

Drizzle vegetables with a light lemon and herb dressing before roasting to bring out their natural sweetness. Toss with tortellini and serve warm or at room temperature for a sensational vegetarian pasta.

Ingredients

1 small eggplant (about 1 pound)
Coarse salt
1 small zucchini (about 8 ounces)
1 small yellow summer squash
   (about 8 ounces)
1 red bell pepper
8 ounces fresh mushrooms
¼ cup extra virgin olive oil
2 tablespoons fresh lemon juice

¼ cup chopped fresh basil, divided
1½ teaspoons chopped fresh thyme
2 cloves garlic, minced
½ teaspoon coarse salt
1 package (9 ounces) fresh cheese
   tortellini
Freshly ground black pepper
Grated Parmesan cheese

Cut eggplant into 1-inch cubes and place in a colander; sprinkle with salt and set aside 30 minutes.

Preheat oven to 425°F. Line a large-rimmed baking sheet with foil. Cut zucchini and squash in half lengthwise and then into ¼-inch-thick slices. Cut pepper into short strips and mushrooms in half. Pat eggplant dry with paper towels. Combine vegetables on prepared baking sheet.

Combine olive oil, lemon juice, 2 tablespoons of the basil, thyme, garlic, and salt in a small bowl. Drizzle oil mixture over vegetables; toss and bake 10 minutes. Stir vegetables; bake 5 to 10 additional minutes or until vegetables are crisp-tender.

While vegetables are roasting, cook tortellini in lightly salted water according to package directions. Drain and toss with vegetables and remaining basil. Season with pepper and toss with Parmesan. Serve warm or at room temperature.

Makes 8 servings

Sausage and Mushroom Dressing

Old-fashioned sausage and mushroom dressing is never out of fashion. It is one of those comfort foods we look forward to at Thanksgiving. This dressing may be your next "must have" Thanksgiving request.

Ingredients

1 to 2 cups (8 to 16 ounces) chicken broth

10 cups (12 ounces) dried bread cubes or croutons

8 ounces bulk pork sausage

4 tablespoons butter

¾ cup chopped onion

8 ounces mushrooms, coarsely chopped

1 teaspoon dried rubbed sage

½ teaspoon salt

¼ teaspoon black pepper

⅛ teaspoon freshly grated nutmeg

⅛ teaspoon ground cinnamon

2 eggs, lightly beaten

Microwave 1 cup of the broth in a 2-cup glass measure on high for 1 minute until warm. Combine bread cubes and warm broth in a large mixing bowl; set aside. Preheat oven to 350°F. Coat a 3-quart baking dish with no-stick cooking spray; set aside.

Cook sausage in a large skillet over medium-high heat stirring often until cooked through. Drain excess fat and crumble sausage with a fork; add to bread. Melt butter in the skillet; add onion and cook stirring often until beginning to get tender. Stir in mushrooms and cook stirring often until tender. Stir in sage, salt, pepper, nutmeg, and cinnamon. Combine mushroom mixture with bread mixture. Adjust seasonings to taste. Add eggs and toss until well mixed. Add additional broth if a more moist dressing is desired.

Spoon dressing into prepared baking dish; cover with foil. Bake 30 minutes; uncover and bake 20 to 30 additional minutes until lightly browned and hot in center.

Makes 10 to 12 servings

CAROL'S TIDBITS

Bread cubes should be made from coarse-textured bread and dried to best absorb broth and not get gummy.

Use your favorite sausage. I like the fennel and garlic in mild Italian sausage, often called sweet Italian sausage.

This dressing may be used to stuff body and neck cavities of a 12 to 18-pound turkey. Dressing should be at room temperature when stuffed in the turkey and baked until dressing is 165°F. Bake extra dressing in a casserole according to the recipe on this page.

Double-Mushroom Bread Pudding

CAROL'S TIDBITS

Remove the dark gills from the underside of portabella caps with a spoon before slicing. The gills are edible, but would give the pudding a muddy appearance.

Bake pudding in ramekins for individual servings. Bake about 20 minutes. A table knife inserted near center should come out clean when puddings are baked.

Bread pudding is not just for dessert. This savory pudding, loaded with mushrooms and cheese, is a wonderful accompaniment to beef entrées and roast turkey.

Ingredients

4 cups milk, divided
1 teaspoon coarse salt, divided
12 cups (about 16 ounces) cubed sourdough or other coarse-textured, lower fat bread
2 tablespoons butter
1 pound baby bella or white button mushrooms, sliced
3 (4-inch) portabella mushroom caps, gills removed, halved and sliced

½ cup chopped fresh parsley
3 cloves garlic, minced
1 tablespoon minced fresh rosemary
½ teaspoon freshly ground black pepper
4 ounces Gruyere cheese, shredded (1 cup)
4 whole eggs
2 egg whites
Chopped fresh parsley for garnish

Combine 2 cups of the milk and ½ teaspoon salt in a large mixing bowl. Add bread cubes and toss until moistened; set aside. Coat a 9x13-inch baking dish with no-stick cooking spray; set aside.

Melt butter in a large skillet over medium-high heat. Stir in mushrooms and cook stirring often until mushrooms begin to soften. Stir in the ½ cup parsley, garlic, rosemary, pepper, and remaining ½ teaspoon salt. Cook 1 minute to blend flavors. Toss mushroom mixture with bread cubes; turn into prepared baking dish. Sprinkle with cheese.

Preheat oven to 375°F. Combine remaining 2 cups milk, eggs, and egg whites in mixing bowl; whisk until blended. Pour egg mixture over bread and mushrooms; let stand 15 minutes.

Bake pudding 35 to 45 minutes or until center of pudding is set. Sprinkle with additional chopped parsley.

Makes 12 servings

DESSERTS

Desserts are one of the great pleasures of life.
These special treats will make a
lasting impression with your guests.

Lemon Blueberry Trifle

The creamy, lemony filling and fresh berries layered with frozen pound cake make a beautiful and delectable trifle. Make the trifle several hours, or even a day, before serving to allow the ingredients to marry.

Ingredients

1 cup granulated sugar
3 tablespoons cornstarch
3 cups milk
4 egg yolks
1 tablespoon plus 1 teaspoon grated lemon peel, divided
4 tablespoons fresh lemon juice
2 cups (1 pint) heavy whipping cream

1 package (10.75 ounces) frozen pound cake, thawed
¼ cup dry sherry
2 cups fresh blueberries
2 tablespoons powdered sugar
Blueberries and lemon peel for garnish

Combine sugar and cornstarch in a medium saucepan; stir in milk and cook over medium heat, stirring constantly, until thickened and smooth. Beat egg yolks in a small bowl and gradually stir in a small amount of hot milk mixture to warm yolks. Stir egg mixture into saucepan and cook stirring constantly just until custard begins to bubble. Remove from heat and stir in the 1 tablespoon lemon peel and lemon juice. Pour into a large metal bowl; cover surface with plastic wrap and chill.

Whip cream in a mixer bowl until stiff. Fold half of the cream into the cooled custard. Chill remaining whipped cream.

Cut pound cake into 1-inch cubes. Arrange half of the cake cubes on the bottom of a 2-quart glass trifle bowl (about 8-inch round bowl). Combine sherry and remaining 1 teaspoon lemon peel; drizzle half of the sherry over cake cubes. Top with 1 cup blueberries and half of the custard. Repeat layers. Stir powdered sugar into remaining whipped cream and spoon onto custard. Garnish with blueberries and lemon peel.

Makes 10 to 12 servings

CAROL'S TIDBITS

Raspberries and blackberries are also delicious with the lemon filling.

Trifles are most inviting when made in a clear glass bowl with straight sides to show off the layers. If trifle bowl is larger than 2-quarts, use two pound cakes.

It is fun to make individual trifles in stemmed wine glasses for an elegant dessert and in simple, funky glasses for casual events. Clear plastic cups even work to take trifles to outdoor concerts and picnics.

12 ounces (1 dry pint) blueberries = 2½ cups

Peach-Blueberry Kuchen

CAROL'S TIDBITS

Use canned or frozen peaches when fresh peaches are not in season.

Many other fruits, especially apples, pears, and plums, make excellent kuchens.

Kuchen is a German cake that is topped with fruit. It is not too sweet for a breakfast coffee cake, but is sweet enough for dessert. Top with fresh peaches and blueberries during peak season and serve with whipped cream. Yum!

Ingredients

½ cup (1 stick) butter, at room temp
¾ cup sugar
2 eggs, at room temp
1 cup flour
1½ teaspoons baking powder
¼ teaspoon salt
1½ teaspoons grated lemon peel

1 tablespoon lemon juice
3 large peaches, peeled and sliced
  (about 24 slices)
1 cup blueberries
½ cup sliced almonds, toasted
3 tablespoons sugar
¾ teaspoon ground cinnamon

Preheat oven to 350°F. Coat a 9-inch springform pan with no-stick cooking spray.

Combine butter and the ¾ cup sugar in a large mixer bowl; beat on medium-high speed until fluffy. Beat in eggs, one at a time, until very smooth and creamy. Add flour, baking powder, salt, lemon peel, and juice; beat on low speed just until blended.

Spread batter in prepared pan. Arrange peach slices over batter; top with blueberries. Combine almonds, the 3 tablespoons sugar, and cinnamon in a small bowl; sprinkle over fruit. Bake 55 to 60 minutes or until lightly browned and wooden pick inserted near center comes out clean. Remove rim of pan just before serving. Serve warm or at room temperature.

Makes 8 servings

Blueberry Galette

If making pies is intimidating, fear no more and make this rustic blueberry free-form tart. Simply roll out the buttery crust, top with sweetened blueberries, fold the edges of the crust over the fruit, and bake. Extra berries sprinkled over the baked galette add a burst of fresh flavor. Delicious served with ice cream!

Ingredients

Crust

1 cup flour

2 teaspoons sugar

¼ teaspoon salt

½ teaspoon ground cinnamon

5 tablespoons cold butter, cubed

3 to 4 tablespoons ice water

Filling

½ cup sugar

2 tablespoons flour

1 tablespoon fresh lemon juice

3 cups blueberries, divided

2 tablespoons sugar, if desired

Combine flour, sugar, salt, and cinnamon in a food processor work bowl. Process with short pulses until mixture is the consistency of coarse crumbs with some butter pieces the size of small peas. Add 3 tablespoons water and pulse until flour is moistened. Add additional water as needed. Shape dough into a flat disc; wrap in plastic wrap and chill 20 to 30 minutes.

Preheat oven to 400°F. Roll dough into a 12-inch round on a lightly floured surface. Transfer to a parchment-lined baking sheet; set aside while making filling.

Combine sugar and flour for filling in a mixing bowl; stir in lemon juice and 2½ cups of the blueberries. Spoon blueberry mixture onto center of crust, leaving a 2-inch border around edge. Gather and fold edge of crust over blueberries; sprinkle with sugar. Bake 35 to 40 minutes or until blueberry juices thicken. Remove from oven and sprinkle remaining ½ cup blueberries over filling.

Makes 6 to 8 servings

CAROL'S TIDBITS

A galette is a French term for a variety of flat, round cakes. They can be made out of pastry dough, yeast dough, even crêpes, and can be either sweet or savory.

For extra flavor pizzazz, stir freshly grated lemon peel into the blueberry mixture.

To make the tart preparation even easier, use a refrigerated pie crust.

Berry Peach Cobbler

CAROL'S TIDBITS

Substitute frozen peaches when fresh peaches are not in season. Measure peaches before completely thawed; toss with sugars and spices. Allow extra time for peaches to thaw and release juice.

Frozen berries may also be used; expect the color of the berries to be more dominent.

A food processor makes quick work cutting butter into the dry ingredients. However, it is best to combine and stir egg into flour mixture in a separate bowl.

I prefer to use peeled peaches although it is not necessary to peel them. To quickly peel peaches, make a small X on the bottom of the fruit and drop it into boiling water for 30 to 60 seconds until the peel begins to curl. Remove fruit with a slotted spoon and immediately drop it into a bowl of ice water. The peel will slip right off with the help of a paring knife.

Is there anything better than peach cobbler? Maybe Berry Peach Cobbler. A buttery, crispy sweet biscuit crust tops peach filling and your choice of blueberries, blackberries, or raspberries to make this a summer classic. Serve with crème fraîche or a generous drizzle of heavy cream.

Ingredients

Fruit

1 cup granulated sugar
¼ cup firmly packed brown sugar
¼ cup flour
½ teaspoon ground cinnamon
¼ teaspoon ground ginger
1 tablespoon lemon juice

1 teaspoon vanilla extract
6 cups (about 6 peaches) sliced peaches
2 cups (12 ounces) blueberries, blackberries, or raspberries

Topping

1¼ cups flour
¼ cup granulated sugar
1 teaspoon baking powder
½ teaspoon salt

½ cup (1 stick) butter, cubed and chilled
1 egg
2 tablespoons milk

Crème Fraîche, if desired (page 169)

Combine sugars, flour, cinnamon, and ginger in a large saucepan; stir to blend well. Stir in lemon juice, vanilla, and peaches; let stand until juice forms and begins to melt sugars.

Preheat oven to 400°F. Coat a shallow 2-quart baking dish with no-stick cooking spray. Combine flour, sugar, baking powder, and salt for topping in a large mixing bowl. Cut in butter with a pastry blender until mixture is consistency of coarse crumbs. Beat egg and milk in a small bowl to blend; stir into flour mixture just until flour is moistened.

Cook peaches over high heat stirring often until boiling; reduce heat to medium and cook until juice thickens. Remove from heat and stir in blueberries. Turn fruit into prepared baking dish sprayed with no-stick cooking spray. Use two small spoons to crumble topping over fruit to look like cobblestones.

Bake 25 to 30 minutes or until topping is golden brown. Serve with Crème Fraîche or heavy whipping cream.

Makes 6 to 8 servings

Strawberry Devonshire Tart

I developed this recipe for a strawberry class many years ago and remains one of my all-time favorite summer desserts. It was submitted to *Country Woman* magazine for a strawberry story. I was honored to have it selected for the story and feature photograph.

Ingredients

Crust

1 cup flour
2 tablespoons sugar
¼ teaspoon salt

6 tablespoons cold butter, cubed
1 egg yolk, lightly beaten
1 tablespoon cold water

Filling and Glaze

1 package (8 ounces) cream cheese, softened
½ cup dairy sour cream
8 tablespoons sugar, divided
2 pounds small strawberries, stems removed

2 cups (8 ounces) frozen raspberries
Water
1 tablespoon cornstarch
Dash salt

Combine flour, sugar, and salt for crust in a mixing bowl; cut in butter with a pastry blender until mixture is the consistency of coarse crumbs. Combine egg yolk and 1 tablespoon cold water; stir into flour until dough forms a ball. Shape dough into a flat disc; wrap in plastic wrap and chill until slightly firm, about 1 hour.

Preheat oven to 400°F. Roll dough into an 11-inch circle between sheets of plastic wrap. Remove top sheet of plastic wrap; invert pastry over a 9-inch tart pan with removable bottom. Gently press pastry onto bottom and up sides of pan; remove plastic wrap. Fold any excess overhanging pastry to inside of pan even with rim and press against side of pan. Pierce bottom and sides of crust to prevent excess shrinking. Bake 12 to 15 minutes or until light brown. Cool.

Combine cream cheese, sour cream, and 3 tablespoons of the sugar for filling in a mixing bowl; blend until smooth. Spread over bottom of cooled cookie crust. Arrange strawberries stem end down over filling.

Combine raspberries and remaining *5* tablespoons of the sugar for glaze in a microwave-safe bowl. Microwave on high for 2 minutes; stir and let stand 15 minutes. Press raspberries through a sieve to remove seeds. Add water to juice to make 1 cup liquid. Stir into cornstarch and salt in a small saucepan; cook stirring constantly over medium heat until thickened and clear. Cool slightly; spoon over strawberries. Chill at least 1 hour.

Makes 8 servings

CAROL'S TIDBITS

Look for uniform size and shaped small berries. The entire 2 pounds will probably not be used, but it is good to have extra berries to select the best. Gently rinse and dry berries before removing stems. Large berries may be sliced and arranged over the filling.

Frozen berries are used for the glaze because freezing causes the berries to give off more juice. Strawberries may also be used for the glaze.

Melted red currant or seedless red raspberry jam can also be used as a glaze.

Serve with a dollop of sweetened whipped cream and a garnish of blueberries for 4th of July celebrations.

White Chocolate Banana Crème Tart

Warm white chocolate in your hand before using a vegetable peeler to make curls or to shave chocolate over the tart.

Bananas are an excellent source of potassium, fiber, and vitamins B6 and C.

Inspired by Southern banana pudding, cheesecake, and white chocolate mousse, this tart has it all. This heavenly dessert is a great winter dessert when bananas are one of our favorite fresh fruits.

Ingredients

1¼ cups vanilla wafer crumbs (35 cookies)
5 tablespoons butter, melted
1 cup (8 ounces) heavy whipping cream, divided
6 ounces white chocolate, divided

1 package (8 ounces) cream cheese, softened
½ cup powdered sugar
2 teaspoons vanilla extract
3 firm, ripe bananas, divided

Preheat oven to 350°F. Combine cookie crumbs and butter until crumbs are moist. Press onto bottom and up sides of a 9-inch tart pan with removable bottom or a 9-inch pie plate. Bake 7 minutes; cool.

Combine ¼ cup of the cream and 4 ounces of the white chocolate in a 2-cup glass measure; microwave on high for 1 minute. Let stand 1 minute; stir until smooth. Cool to room temperature.

Beat cream cheese, powdered sugar, and vanilla in a large mixer bowl until smooth. Add cooled white chocolate mixture and remaining ¾ cup cream; beat until fluffy. Spread half of the cheese filling over crust. Slice 2 bananas and arrange over filling. Spread remaining filling over bananas. Shave remaining 2 ounces white chocolate over filling. Chill tart for at least 3 hours. Garnish with remaining sliced banana before serving.

Makes 8 to 10 servings

Homemade Pie Crust

Making pie crust can be easy as pie when you follow these tips!

Ingredients

Single Crust:

1½ cups flour
½ teaspoon salt
¼ cup cold butter, cubed

¼ cup solid vegetable shortening, chilled and cubed
4 to 5 tablespoons ice water

Double Crust:

2½ cups flour
1 teaspoon salt
½ cup cold butter, cubed

6 tablespoons solid vegetable shortening, chilled and cubed
5 to 7 tablespoons ice water

Combine flour and salt in a large mixing bowl. Cut in butter and shortening with a pastry blender until mixture is the consistency of coarse crumbs with some butter pieces the size of small peas. Sprinkle with minimum amount of water; quickly stir until dough begins to clump together. Add additional water if dough is dry. Form dough into a disc (2 discs if making a double crust); wrap in plastic wrap and chill for 30 minutes. Roll disc on a lightly floured surface or between 2 large sheets of plastic wrap until ⅛-inch thick. Begin rolling in the center of the disc, roll to the outside edges and lift the rolling pin before rolling over the edge. Rotate the dough a quarter turn after each rolling to keep the disc round. Fit pastry into a pie plate.

If preparing dough in a food processor: Combine flour, salt, butter, and shortening in a food processor work bowl fitted with steel knife blade. Pulse just until mixture is the consistency of coarse crumbs with some butter pieces the size of peas. Sprinkle with minimum amount of water and pulse just until dough begins to clump together, adding additional water as needed. Do not process until dough forms into a ball or the crust will be tough. Shape, chill, and roll as above.

If making a single crust pie, trim crust ½ to 1 inch beyond edge of pie plate. Fold dough under and flute edge. Bake according to your pie recipe directions.

If prebaking a single crust, refrigerate pie crust in pie plate for 30 minutes. Pierce bottom and sides of crust with tines of a fork. Line bottom and sides with heavy duty foil pressed firmly against the dough. Bake at 425°F for 10 minutes. Remove foil and bake 5 additional minutes until dry and lightly browned.

If making a double crust pie, trim bottom crust fitted into pie plate even with rim. Add filling. Trim top crust ½ inch beyond rim and tuck under edge of bottom crust. Flute crust edge. Cut vents in top crust. Bake according to your pie recipe directions.

Kentucky Pecan Pie

CAROL'S TIDBITS

See page 157 for a homemade pie crust recipe or use a refrigerated pie crust.

Bourbon is a corn-based whiskey named after Bourbon County, Kentucky. The whiskey can be made anywhere in the United States, but is most strongly associated with Kentucky.

Very cold cream, mixer bowl, and beaters will help cream whip quickly and will increase the volume.

Chocolate chips and a splash of bourbon are the special ingredients in this classic Kentucky pecan pie.

Ingredients

¾ cup sugar
¼ cup flour
Dash salt
½ cup (1 stick) butter, melted
2 eggs
2 tablespoons bourbon, divided
1 cup (6 ounces) semisweet chocolate chips

1 cup pecan pieces
1 (9-inch) unbaked pie crust
1 cup (8 ounces) heavy whipping cream
2 tablespoons powdered sugar
Chocolate shavings

Preheat oven to 350°F. Combine sugar, flour, and salt in a mixing bowl; blend in butter, eggs, and 1 tablespoon of the bourbon. Stir in chocolate pieces and pecans. Fit crust into a 9-inch pie plate. Pour filling into pie crust; bake on bottom oven shelf 30 to 35 minutes or until knife inserted near center comes out clean. Cool on wire rack.

Whip cream with powdered sugar and the remaining tablespoon of bourbon in a large mixer bowl until stiff. Garnish pie with whipped cream and sprinkle with chocolate shavings.

Makes 8 servings

Note: For a more crispy crust, partially bake pie shell before adding filling. Preheat oven to 425°F. Line the bottom and sides of the pie shell with heavy duty foil, pressing foil firmly against dough. Bake 10 minutes. Remove foil; cool. Add filling and bake according to recipe directions. Cover edge of crust with foil if it becomes too brown.

Apple Praline Pie

The ultimate apple pie! America's favorite dessert is glazed with a buttery praline topping of brown sugar and pecans that seeps into the apple filling. Served with ice cream, this truly is a slice of heaven.

Ingredients

Pastry for 2-crust pie
6 cups peeled and thinly sliced apples, about 6 apples
¾ cup granulated sugar

¼ cup flour
1 teaspoon ground cinnamon
⅛ teaspoon salt

Praline Topping
6 tablespoons butter
6 tablespoons dark brown sugar

1½ tablespoons half-and-half
⅓ cup chopped pecans

Preheat oven to 350°F. Place one crust in a 9-inch deep-dish pie plate.

Place sliced apples in a large mixing bowl. Combine granulated sugar, flour, cinnamon and salt; sprinkle over apples and toss until all apples are coated. Spoon apples into pie crust. Top with second crust and make a high fluted edge. Cut large slits in top crust to let steam escape and praline topping soak into apple filling.

Place pie on a large sheet of foil. Bake on bottom oven shelf 60 to 65 minutes or until apples are tender and juices are thickened.

Meanwhile, combine butter, brown sugar, and half-and-half in a small saucepan; bring to a full boil stirring constantly. Remove from heat; stir in pecans and spread over warm pie. Return pie to oven and bake until topping bubbles, about 5 minutes. Cool at least 1 hour before serving. Serve with vanilla ice cream.

Makes 8 to 12 servings.

CAROL'S TIDBITS

To prevent excessive browning, cover crust edge with foil after 20 minutes of baking.

Braeburn apples are my apple of choice for pie. Choose apples that are crisp, sweet-tart, and hold up during baking. Granny Smith is a popular choice, but I prefer to blend them with slightly sweeter Braeburn or Pink Lady. Other good pie baking apples are Jonathan, Jonagold, Pippin, Gravenstein, and Golden Delicious.

Red Delicious, Gala, Fuji, and Courtland tend to get mushy or black when baked.

Make your own pie crust (page 157) if you prefer, but this is an excellent time to use refrigerated pie crusts.

White Chocolate Chunk Brownies with Caramel Sauce

CAROL'S TIDBITS

Look for espresso powder in the coffee aisle.

Brownies may also be baked in a 9-inch square pan. For thinner brownies, use a 9x13-inch pan.

Toast pecans in a shallow pan in a 300 °F oven for about 10 minutes or in a skillet over low heat, stirring often.

Blondie brownies is the name given to brownies made with brown sugar and no chocolate.

A dash of salt added to caramel sauces will mellow the sweetness.

Chunks of white chocolate and pecans in a moist, coffee-flavored blondie brownie make a winning taste combination. For the piece de resistance, top with a scoop of ice cream and Brown Sugar Caramel Sauce.

Ingredients

3 tablespoons instant espresso powder
1 tablespoon warm water
2 cups firmly packed dark brown sugar
¾ cup (1½ sticks) butter
2 eggs
2 tablespoons coffee liqueur
2 cups flour

2 teaspoons baking powder
½ teaspoon salt
4 ounces white chocolate, cut into
  ¾-inch pieces
¾ cup coarsely chopped toasted
  pecans
Vanilla ice cream

Preheat oven to 350 °F. Coat a 10-inch cake or springform pan with no-stick cooking spray and line bottom with parchment paper.

Combine espresso powder and water in a large saucepan; stir until dissolved. Add brown sugar and butter; stir over medium heat until butter melts. Remove from heat and cool 5 minutes. Whisk in eggs and coffee liqueur. Stir in flour, baking powder, and salt until well blended. Stir in white chocolate and pecans. Spread in prepared pan. Bake 35 to 40 minutes or until wooden pick inserted near center comes out clean.

Cool before cutting into wedges and serving with ice cream and Brown Sugar Caramel Sauce.

Makes 16 servings

Brown Sugar Caramel Sauce

8 tablespoons (1 stick) butter
1 cup firmly packed dark brown sugar
½ cup (4 ounces) heavy whipping cream

½ teaspoon vanilla extract
Dash salt

Melt butter in a small saucepan over medium heat. Add brown sugar and cook stirring often until mixture comes to a boil. Gradually add cream; cook whisking often until mixture comes to a boil. Remove from heat. Stir in vanilla and salt. Serve warm.

Makes 1½ cups sauce

Grand Marnier Chocolate Cobbler

Chocolate lovers, this is your dessert. Its soufflé-like appearance is impressive, and underneath a tender chocolate cake topping is a very rich, fudgy pudding. Skip dinner and go right to dessert!

Ingredients

Cobbler Base

½ cup (1 stick) butter

6 ounces semisweet chocolate, chopped

2 eggs, lightly beaten

¼ cup Grand Marnier liqueur

2 tablespoons sugar

Cobbler Topping

½ cup sugar

½ cup flour

2 tablespoons unsweetened cocoa powder

½ teaspoon baking powder

¼ cup milk

3 tablespoons butter, melted

2 tablespoons Grand Marnier liqueur

¼ cup boiling water

Raspberry sauce

Ice cream

Fresh raspberries

Coat six ¾-cup ramekins with no-stick cooking spray. Combine butter and chocolate in a microwave-safe mixing bowl. Microwave on high stirring every 30 seconds until chocolate is melted and smooth. Combine eggs, liqueur, and sugar in a small bowl; blend until smooth. Add to chocolate mixture and stir until well blended. Divide evenly among ramekins. Chill for 30 minutes or until chocolate is slightly firm.

Preheat oven to 375°F. Combine sugar, flour, cocoa powder, and baking powder for topping. Stir in milk, melted butter, and liqueur until blended. Stir in boiling water. Pour batter over chocolate mixture in each ramekin. Bake 20 to 22 minutes or until cobbler topping puffs up and cracks. Serve warm with ice cream, raspberry sauce, and fresh raspberries.

Makes 6 desserts

CAROL'S TIDBITS

Look for prepared raspberry dessert sauces in the produce department or with ice cream toppings.

To make ahead, prepare and chill the base layer; it can chill longer than 30 minutes. Have topping ingredients ready to mix after dinner. Enjoy a cup of coffee while the desserts bake.

Chilling the base layer keeps the topping separate and it ensures that the base will still be fudgy after baking.

Grand Marnier is an orange-flavored brandy liqueur. Other liqueurs may be used.

Cobbler may be baked in 12 foil cupcake liners set in muffin cups; bake 18 to 20 minutes.

Macadamia Fudge Cake

CAROL'S TIDBITS

Espresso powder is often added to chocolate desserts to enhance the chocolate and give the dessert a richer more intense flavor.

Whole macadamia nuts are too big in the sauce. Chopped macadamia nuts are too small and powdery. Macadamia nuts cut in half with a knife are just right.

Macadamia nuts are high in fat. It is best to store them in the refrigerator to prevent rancidity (if they last that long).

This fudgy one-bowl, one-layer cake has the texture of cake and the flavor of brownies. It is best served with ice cream. It is birthday cake at our house.

Ingredients

Cake
¾ cup sugar
½ cup (1 stick) butter, softened
¾ cup dairy sour cream
1 egg, at room temp
½ teaspoon vanilla extract
1 cup flour

¼ cup unsweetened cocoa powder
1½ teaspoons instant
  espresso powder
½ teaspoon baking powder
½ teaspoon baking soda
¼ teaspoon salt

Macadamia Fudge Topping
1 cup (8 ounces) heavy whipping
  cream
½ cup sugar
4 ounces semisweet chocolate, chopped

2 tablespoons butter
1 tablespoon light corn syrup
1 teaspoon vanilla extract
1 cup macadamia nuts, halved

For cake: Preheat oven to 350°F. Coat a 9-inch round cake pan with no-stick spray and line bottom with parchment paper.

Combine sugar and butter in a large mixer bowl; beat on medium speed until creamy. Add sour cream, egg, vanilla, flour, cocoa powder, espresso powder, baking powder, baking soda, and salt; beat on low speed just until blended.

Pour batter into prepared pan. Bake 30 to 35 minutes or until wooden pick inserted near center comes out clean. Cool cake in pan on a wire rack for 10 minutes. Remove cake from pan and cool completely.

For Macadamia Fudge Topping: Combine cream, sugar, chocolate, butter, and corn syrup in a medium saucepan; cook over medium-high heat stirring constantly until mixture comes to a boil. Reduce heat and cook for 5 minutes, stirring often. Remove from heat; stir in vanilla.

To serve: Drizzle ½ cup topping over cake before adding nuts. Cut cake into wedges. Serve cake wedges with a scoop of ice cream; stir nuts into remaining topping and spoon over cake and ice cream.

Makes 10 to 12 servings

Sticky Toffee Pudding

Pudding is a British term for dessert. This classic English dessert is really a buttery date cake served with a warm toffee sauce. The dessert's origin is a mystery although many claim to have invented it over a century ago. It is popular in this country as well and is served at many restaurants and pubs.

Ingredients

1 package (8 ounces) pitted dates, finely chopped
1 cup water
¾ teaspoon baking soda
1 cup (2 sticks) butter, divided
1 cup granulated sugar
2 eggs
1 teaspoon vanilla extract

1⅓ cups flour
½ teaspoon baking powder
⅛ teaspoon salt
1 cup firmly packed brown sugar
1 cup (8 ounces) heavy whipping cream
Whipped cream or ice cream

Preheat oven to 350°F. Coat eight to ten 4-ounce ramekins or custard cups with no-stick cooking spray; set on a shallow baking pan.

Combine dates and water in a medium saucepan; bring to a boil over medium-high heat. Remove from heat and stir in baking soda (mixture will foam); set aside to cool.

Combine ½ cup of the butter and granulated sugar in a large mixer bowl; beat on medium-high speed until fluffy. Beat in eggs, one at a time, beating until creamy and thickened. Stir in vanilla and date mixture. Combine flour, baking powder, and salt; add to date mixture and stir just until blended.

Divide batter evenly among prepared ramekins. Bake 25 to 30 minutes or until wooden pick inserted near center comes out clean. Cool on a wire rack for 5 minutes before unmolding cakes.

Combine brown sugar and remaining ½ cup butter in a medium saucepan; cook over medium heat until mixture is bubbly and sugar is dissolved. Stir in cream and cook until slightly thickened. Poke holes in the surface of the cakes with a fork or skewer. Spoon toffee sauce over cakes and serve with whipped cream or ice cream.

Makes 8 to 10 servings

CAROL'S TIDBITS

The baking soda tenderizes the dates and makes a moist, rich dessert; it will be difficult to identify any dates in the baked cake.

The cake may be made with either granulated or brown sugar. I use granulated sugar for a more delicate flavored cake and greater flavor contrast with the brown sugar toffee sauce.

A friend living in London blogged that Sticky Toffee Pudding was one of her "favorite English food discoveries."

Sharrow Bay Hotel in England's Lake District refined a recipe originally called "icky, sticky toffee sponge" and now sells a retail version of this dessert.

Frosty Mocha Meringue Pie

CAROL'S TIDBITS

Be sure to use a metal pie plate because the pie will go from freezer to hot oven.

Use your favorite ice creams and ice cream sauces.

To produce the best volume meringue, begin beating egg whites on low speed until foamy. Gradually increase speed to high and beat until soft peaks before adding sugar.

Summer begs for ice cream desserts and this baked Alaska pie is your answer. Don't let the number of steps scare you as this is very easy to prepare and can be done many days before serving. Crunchy pecan crust, ice cream, fudge sauce and toasted meringue that tastes like toasted marshmallows; what's not to love?

Ingredients

Pecan Crust

1 egg white, at room temp
Dash salt
¼ cup sugar
1½ cups finely chopped pecans

Fudge Sauce

1 package (6 ounces) semisweet chocolate chips
½ cup water
¼ cup sugar
¼ cup light corn syrup
1 tablespoon butter
1 teaspoon vanilla extract
Dash salt

Filling

1½ quarts coffee ice cream
1 pint chocolate ice cream

Meringue

3 egg whites, at room temp
½ teaspoon vanilla extract
¼ teaspoon cream of tartar
6 tablespoons sugar

For pecan crust: Preheat oven to 400°F. Butter and flour a 9-inch metal pie plate. Beat egg white and salt in a small mixer bowl until soft peaks form; gradually beat in sugar until stiff peaks form. Fold in pecans.

Spread mixture in prepared pie plate, pressing mixture against sides with back of fork. Bake 10 minutes; cool completely.

Continued, next page

For fudge sauce: Combine chocolate chips, water, sugar, and corn syrup in a medium microwave-safe bowl. Microwave on high for 2 minutes, stirring once. Stir in butter, vanilla, and salt; microwave 1 additional minute. Stir until smooth. Cool completely. (Sauce thickens as it cools.)

For filling: Scoop half of the coffee ice cream into the cooled pecan crust; drizzle ½ cup fudge sauce over ice cream. Scoop chocolate ice cream onto coffee ice cream layer; drizzle with ½ cup fudge sauce. Scoop remaining coffee ice cream onto chocolate ice cream layer; drizzle with ½ cup fudge sauce. Freeze pie for at least 2 hours until ice cream is very firm.

For meringue: Preheat oven to 425°F. Beat egg whites, vanilla, and cream of tartar in a small mixer bowl until soft peaks form; gradually beat in sugar until stiff peaks form. Spread meringue over frozen pie, completely covering ice cream and sealing meringue to crust. Bake until meringue is golden brown, about 3 to 5 minutes. Return pie to freezer; freeze until firm.

Makes 8 servings

Dark Chocolate Sauce

Chocoholics will love the intense chocolate flavor of this sauce. Serve it with Mississippi Mud Dessert Squares (page 166).

Ingredients

1 cup (8 ounces) heavy whipping cream	⅓ cup firmly packed dark brown sugar
2 tablespoons butter	1 teaspoon espresso powder
½ cup unsweetened cocoa powder	Dash salt
⅓ cup granulated sugar	

Combine all ingredients in a small saucepan. Cook stirring often over medium heat until mixture comes to a boil and sugars are dissolved. Serve warm or at room temperature. Store sauce in refrigerator.

Makes 1 cup sauce

Mississippi Mud Dessert Squares

CAROL'S TIDBITS

Ice cream packaged in square cartons works the very best to slice and arrange on the brownie layer.

Try other ice creams and liqueurs that pair well with chocolate.

Mississippi Mud is the name given to many brownies, pies, cakes, and desserts. The origin of the name is not known, but some sources say one of the recipes originated in the state of Mississippi; others say it is because many of the desserts look like the muddy banks of the Mississippi River.

This recipe was adapted from the Mississippi Mud Pie served on the Delta Queen steamboat when it cruised on the Mississippi River. It is now moored in Chattanooga, Tennessee and has been converted into a floating hotel.

Chocolate is always the star ingredient in any Mississippi Mud dessert. This time it stars in the brownies, ice cream, whipped cream, and chocolate sauce. It is sure to satisfy every chocolate lover's sweet tooth.

Ingredients

Chocolate Brownie
1 cup (2 sticks) butter
2 cups granulated sugar
¼ teaspoon salt
4 eggs

1 teaspoon vanilla extract
4 ounces unsweetened chocolate, melted and cooled
1 cup flour
1 cup chopped pecans, if desired

Ice Cream
2 quarts chocolate ice cream, sliced

Whipped Cream
1½ cups (12 ounces) heavy whipping cream
½ cup powdered sugar

2 tablespoons crème de cacao or chocolate liqueur

Dark Chocolate Sauce (page 165)

Preheat oven to 375°F. Line a 9x13-inch baking pan with parchment or foil.

Combine butter, granulated sugar, salt, eggs, and vanilla in a large mixer bowl; beat on medium-high speed until fluffy. Stir in chocolate and flour until well blended. Stir in pecans. Spread in prepared baking pan. Bake 25 to 30 minutes or until wooden pick inserted near center comes out clean. Cool to room temperature; chill in freezer.

Top brownies with slices of ice cream; place in freezer. Whip cream with powdered sugar in a large mixer bowl until stiff. Blend in liqueur and spread over ice cream layer. Cover and freeze overnight. Cut into squares and serve with Dark Chocolate Sauce.

Makes 12 to 15 servings

Almond-Crusted Lemon Pound Cake

An already delicious lemon pound cake gets an extra bonus with a sugared almond crust. Serve the cake with fresh fruit and Lemon Crème Fraîche.

Ingredients

1 tablespoon butter, softened
½ cup sliced almonds
1 cup (2 sticks) butter, at room temp
2 cups sugar
1 tablespoon grated lemon peel
1 tablespoon vanilla extract
4 eggs, at room temp

3 cups flour
½ teaspoon baking powder
½ teaspoon baking soda
¼ teaspoon salt
1 cup (8 ounces) buttermilk
Fresh berries or peaches

Lemon Crème Fraîche

1 cup (8 ounces) heavy whipping cream

1 carton (6 ounces) lemon yogurt
1 tablespoon grated lemon peel

Preheat oven to 350°F. Coat inside of a 10-inch tube pan with 1 tablespoon softened butter; sprinkle with almonds and set aside. Beat 1 cup butter in a large mixer bowl on medium-high speed until creamy. Gradually beat in sugar until light and fluffy. Add lemon peel and vanilla. Beat in eggs, one at a time, and beating well on medium speed after each addition. Combine flour, baking powder, baking soda, and salt. Add flour to butter mixture alternately with buttermilk beginning and ending with flour, beating on low speed just until blended after each addition.

Pour batter into prepared pan. Bake 55 to 65 minutes or until wooden pick inserted near center comes out clean. Cool cake 10 minutes; remove from pan and cool completely a wire rack. Serve with fruit and Lemon Crème Fraîche.

For crème fraîche: Combine cream and yogurt in a non-metal container; let stand loosely covered at room temperature up to 6 hours or until thickened. Stir in lemon peel; chill.

Makes one 10-cake and 1¾ cups crème fraîche

Rum Cake with Pineapple and Crème Anglaise

CAROL'S TIDBITS

Glazed rum cake can get sticky and be difficult to transfer from the wire rack to the serving plate. To make this easier, place Bundt pan over glazed cake and invert cake back into the pan. Then, invert cake onto serving plate. Voila!

This buttery, rum-soaked cake will put you in a Caribbean mood very quickly. Serve it with a custard sauce and fresh pineapple for a festive occasion.

Ingredients

Cake

¾ cup (1½ sticks) butter, at room temp
1¾ cups sugar
2 eggs, at room temp
1½ teaspoons vanilla extract

3 cups flour
2½ teaspoons baking powder
¾ teaspoon salt
1¼ cups milk

Rum Syrup

½ cup (1 stick) butter
1 cup sugar

¼ cup water
¼ cup dark rum

Fresh Pineapple, Cubed

Crème Anglaise (recipe next page)

Preheat oven to 350°F. Coat a 12-cup Bundt pan with no-stick cooking spray. Beat the ¾ cup butter in a large mixer bowl on medium-high speed until creamy. Gradually add the 1¾ cups sugar and beat until light. Beat in eggs, one at a time, and vanilla until light and fluffy. Combine flour, baking powder, and salt. Add to creamed mixture alternately with milk. Beat on low speed for 1 minute until smooth.

Spoon batter into prepared pan. Bake 50 to 60 minutes or until wooden pick inserted near center comes out clean. Cool cake in pan on a wire rack for 10 minutes; invert cake onto the rack set over a shallow tray. Poke cake repeatedly with a long-tined fork or skewer.

Melt the ½ cup butter in a small saucepan over medium heat. Stir in the sugar and water; increase heat to high and cook, stirring often until sugar dissolves. Remove from heat and stir in rum. Spoon rum syrup over cake until all of the syrup is absorbed.

Serve cake with fresh pineapple and Crème Anglaise (on following page).

Makes 12 to 16 servings

Crème Anglaise

2 cups (16 ounces) half-and-half
¼ cup sugar
1 teaspoon cornstarch
3 egg yolks

1½ to 2 tablespoons almond or
   hazelnut liqueur
¼ teaspoon vanilla extract

Rinse a medium saucepan with cold water. Add cream and heat over medium heat just until ready to boil. Combine sugar and cornstarch in a small mixer bowl; add egg yolks and beat on high speed until pale yellow and beginning to thicken. Reduce speed to low and slowly add hot cream in a steady stream. Return mixture to the saucepan and cook over low heat stirring constantly until mixture begins to thicken and coats a metal spoon. Remove from heat; stir in liqueur and vanilla. Chill before serving.

Makes 2 cups sauce

CAROL'S TIDBITS

Anglaise is French for "in the English style;" crème anglaise (English Cream) is the French translation for custard sauce.

Crème Fraîche

Creamy and rich, crème fraîche is a thickened cream with a slightly tangy flavor. It is the finishing touch that makes many desserts, especially fruit desserts really delicious.

Ingredients

1 cup (8 ounces) heavy whipping cream
2 tablespoons buttermilk

Sugar, if desired

Combine cream and buttermilk in a 2-cup glass measure; cover with a paper towel and let stand at room temperature for 24 hours or until thickened. Chill before serving. Crème fraîche may be sweetened with sugar to taste.

Makes 1 cup

CAROL'S TIDBITS

Crème fraîche must be made at least a day before serving.

Carrot Cake
with Cream Cheese Crème

Carrot cake is always a crowd pleaser. This recipe uses cooked carrots for a more consistent, pound cake-like texture and is baked in a Bundt pan for a more elegant appearance. It is served with a rich cream cheese topping that is less sweet than traditional icing.

Ingredients

3 cups flour
2½ cups sugar
1 tablespoon ground cinnamon
2 teaspoons baking soda
1 teaspoon salt
1 can (8 ounces) crushed pineapple, undrained

4 eggs, lightly beaten
1⅓ cups puréed cooked carrots
1 cup vegetable oil
1 tablespoon vanilla extract
1½ cups walnuts, chopped
1½ cups sweetened flaked coconut
Powdered sugar for garnish

Preheat oven to 350°F. Coat a 12-cup Bundt pan with no-stick cooking spray. Combine flour, sugar, cinnamon, baking soda, and salt on wax paper; set aside. Drain pineapple, reserving juice. Place crushed pineapple in a 1-cup measure; add enough reserved juice to make ¾ cup; discard remaining juice. Combine eggs, carrots, oil, pineapple, and vanilla in a large mixing bowl. Stir in flour mixture, walnuts, and coconut.

Pour batter into prepared pan. Bake for 60 to 70 minutes or until edges have pulled away from sides and a wooden pick inserted near center comes out clean. Cool on a wire rack for 10 minutes. Remove cake from pan and cool completely. Sprinkle powdered sugar over cake. Serve with Cream Cheese Crème.

Cream Cheese Crème

1 package (8 ounces) cream cheese, softened

⅓ cup powdered sugar 1 cup (8 ounces) heavy whipping cream

Blend cream cheese and sugar in a large mixer bowl on low speed until smooth. Gradually beat in heavy cream on medium speed until desired consistency is reached. Serve slightly chilled.

Makes 2 cups sauce

Gingerbread Cake with Caramelized Pears

Puréed fresh pear adds moistness and sophistication to this gingerbread pound cake. Serve the cake alone, or as a shortcake with whipped cream and caramelized pears.

Ingredients

3 cups flour
1 teaspoon baking soda
1 teaspoon ground ginger
1 teaspoon ground cinnamon
½ teaspoon salt
½ teaspoon ground allspice
½ teaspoon ground cloves
½ cup puréed pear (about 1 ripe pear)

½ cup buttermilk
1 cup (2 sticks) butter, at room temp
1 cup firmly packed brown sugar
3 eggs, at room temp
¾ cup molasses
Sweetened whipped cream

Caramelized Pears

3 tablespoons butter
4 firm pears, cut into ¼-inch slices

6 tablespoons sugar
Dash salt

Preheat oven to 350°F. Coat a 12-cup Bundt or 10-inch tube pan with no-stick cooking spray. Combine flour, baking powder, ginger, cinnamon, salt, allspice, and cloves; set aside. Combine puréed pear and buttermilk in a 1-cup glass measure; set aside.

Combine butter and brown sugar in a large mixer bowl; beat on medium-high speed until fluffy. Beat in eggs, one at a time and beating well after each addition. Beat in molasses. (Molasses may give batter a curdled appearance.) Add flour mixture alternately with pear mixture, blending on low speed.

Turn batter into prepared pan. Bake 50 to 60 minutes or until wooden pick inserted near center comes out clean. Cool cake in pan on a wire rack for 10 minutes. Remove cake from pan. Cake may be served warm or at room temperature.

For pears: Melt butter in a large nonstick skillet over medium-high heat until butter sizzles. Add pear slices; cook until pears begin to brown, about 5 minutes. Sprinkle sugar and salt over pears and cook stirring often until golden caramel in color. Remove pears from heat and cool to room temperature for best flavor.

Serve cake with sweetened whipped cream and Caramelized Pears.

Makes 16 servings

CAROL'S TIDBITS

Applesauce may be substituted for the puréed pear.

Molasses gets its name from the Latin word for "honey." My favorite molasses in any recipe is Grandma's Molasses Original.

Bartlett, the most common pear variety, is often used for canned pears and is a good choice for puréeing.

Bosc pears have a cinnamon-brown skin and long necks. Their firmer texture and honey-like flavor makes them a good choice for caramelizing.

Anjou pears are good, all-around eating and cooking pears.

Add minced crystallized ginger to sweetened whipped cream for extra delicious flavor.

Gingered Apple Crisp

CAROL'S TIDBITS

Use Granny Smith apples if you like tart apples. Use Golden Delicious apples it you like mild apples. For flavorful apples in between tart and mild, use Braeburn, Jonathan, Gala, Pink Lady, or Fugi. A mixture of different apples combines the best of many flavors and textures.

A shallow 2-quart baking dish may be substituted for a 9x13-inch baking dish.

Apple crisp is a comfort food dessert that is especially scrumptious in the autumn when fresh apples are abundant. Crystallized ginger adds pizzazz to the crisp topping and be sure to serve it with caramel or vanilla ice cream.

Ingredients

10 large tart apples, peeled and thinly sliced (about 12 cups)
2 tablespoons lemon juice
1¼ cups flour
¾ cup granulated sugar

¾ cup firmly packed brown sugar
¾ cup (1½ sticks) butter, cubed and chilled
¼ cup (2 ounces) finely chopped crystallized ginger

Preheat oven to 375°F. Coat a 9x13-inch baking pan with no-stick cooking spray. Toss apple slices with lemon juice in a large bowl; arrange in baking dish.

Combine flour and sugars in a mixing bowl; cut in butter with a pastry blender or electric mixer until butter is the size of small peas. Add ginger and mix until mixture resembles coarse crumbs. Sprinkle mixture evenly over apples.

Bake until topping is golden brown and apple juices are bubbling, about 45 minutes. Serve warm or at room temperature with caramel or vanilla ice cream.

Makes 10 to 12 servings

Cinnamon-Pecan Bread Pudding

Bread puddings are a great way to use stale bread. This pudding combines French bread and flaky croissants, but can be made with just one of the breads. Cinnamon, dried cranberries, and pecans add interest, but the combination of a warm caramel sauce and a cold custard sauce make this bread pudding unforgettable.

Ingredients

½ cup milk
1 tablespoon ground cinnamon
3 eggs
2 egg yolks
⅔ cup firmly packed brown sugar
2 cups half-and-half
2 cups 1-inch cubes
   French bread (3 to 4 ounces)
2 cups 1-inch cubes croissants
   (about 5 ounces or 2 croissants)

¾ sweetened dried cranberries
¾ cup chopped pecans
2 tablespoons firmly packed brown
   sugar
Brown Sugar Caramel Sauce
   (page 160)
Crème Anglaise custard sauce
   (page 169)

Brown Sugar Caramel Sauce (page 160)
Crème Anglaise custard sauce (page 169)

Combine milk and cinnamon in a 1-cup glass measure; microwave on high for 1 minute to warm milk and blend in cinnamon. Set aside to cool. Whisk eggs, egg yolks, and brown sugar in a large bowl until blended. Whisk in milk mixture. Spread bread and croissant cubes in an 8x8x2-inch baking dish that has been coated with no-stick cooking spray; sprinkle with cranberries. Pour egg mixture over bread. Let stand for 30 minutes for bread to absorb egg mixture.

Preheat oven to 350°F. Sprinkle pecans and brown sugar over top; bake until pudding is puffed and firm in the center, about 40 minutes. Serve warm with caramel and/or custard sauces.

Makes 8 servings

CAROL'S TIDBITS

Remove any thick crust from French bread before cubing.

If bread is very fresh, spread cubed bread on a tray to dry a bit before combining with egg mixture.

Raisins may be substituted for dried cranberries.

For extra special flavor, add 2 tablespoons brandy to Brown Sugar Caramel Sauce.

Baked
Amaretti-Stuffed Pears

CAROL'S TIDBITS

Amaretti are flavored with bitter-almond paste or apricot kernel paste. Look for them in the specialty cookie section or at Italian markets.

Crisp ginger cookies may be substituted for amaretti.

Pears can be baked the day before and refrigerated. Warm pears in oven until glaze on pears is melted and sauce is bubbly. Drizzle with chocolate.

I like to use Bosc pears for this dessert.

Amaretti are crisp, almond-flavored Italian macaroons that add a surprise center to baked pears. Another surprise is the caramel sauce that forms as the pears bake.

Ingredients

¾ cup sugar
1 cup coarsely crushed amaretti cookies
2 tablespoons brandy
6 firm ripe pears
1½ cups (12 ounces) heavy whipping cream, divided

2 tablespoons vanilla extract
1½ teaspoons almond extract
1 to 2 ounces semisweet or bittersweet chocolate, melted
½ cup sliced almonds, toasted

Preheat oven to 350°F. Coat a 9x13-inch baking dish with no-stick cooking spray and spread sugar evenly over bottom of dish.

Combine cookie crumbs and brandy; set aside. Peel pears, leaving stems intact. Use a melon ball cutter to hollow out cores from the bottom. Fill pear cavities with crumb mixture. Place pears upright in baking dish. Combine 6 tablespoons of the heavy cream with vanilla and almond extracts; drizzle over the pears.

Bake pears until sugar is a golden color, about 25 to 30 minutes. Pour remaining cream over pears and stir into melted sugar. Return pears to oven; bake 15 minutes. Stir and baste pears with cream mixture. Continue to bake until pears are tender and lightly browned, about 15 additional minutes.

To serve, place pears on serving plates. Spoon sauce over pears. Drizzle pears with melted chocolate. Sprinkle with toasted almonds or additional crushed Amaretti cookies.

Makes 6 servings

Warm Apple Bread Pudding with a Pecan Praline Crust

Bread pudding is a simple, delicious way to use leftover bread. Apples and cinnamon add flavor and crumbled pecan cookies add texture to this bread pudding to make it extra delicious. Add caramel sauce and it is over-the-top delicious.

Ingredients

- ½ loaf (about 8 ounces) white or cinnamon swirl bread
- 2 tablespoons butter
- 2 Golden Delicious or Granny Smith apples, peeled and finely chopped
- 8 tablespoons sugar, divided
- ½ teaspoon ground cinnamon
- 1½ cups milk
- 2 eggs
- 1 egg yolk (reserve white for Pecan Praline Cookies)
- Pecan Praline Cookie crumbs (recipe follows), if desired
- Caramel sauce, if desired

Preheat oven to 300°F. Coat an 8-inch square baking dish with no-stick cooking spray. Cut bread into 1-inch pieces; spread in single layer on rimmed baking sheet. Bake 10 minutes; cool. Increase temperature to 350°F.

Melt butter in a large skillet over medium-high heat. Stir in apples and 2 tablespoons of the sugar; cook, stirring often until apples are tender, about 10 minutes. Cool.

Combine remaining 6 tablespoons sugar and cinnamon in a medium bowl. Stir in milk, eggs and egg yolk; whisk until well blended. Pour over bread cubes and let stand 15 minutes occasionally pressing lightly on the bread to absorb the milk mixture. Bake 40 minutes or until knife inserted near center comes out clean. Serve warm with crumbled cookies and caramel sauce.

Makes 6 to 8 servings

Pecan Praline Cookies

- 4 tablespoons butter, melted
- 1¼ cups chopped pecans
- ½ cup sugar
- 2½ tablespoons flour
- 1 egg white (reserved from bread pudding)

Preheat oven to 350°F. Line a baking sheet with parchment paper. Combine all ingredients in a bowl and blend well. Drop dough by heaping teaspoonfuls onto prepared baking sheet and spread forming 12 thin cookies. Bake until light brown in center, about 10 to 15 minutes. Cool cookies on parchment. Crumble cookies to sprinkle over pudding.

CAROL'S TIDBITS

Choose coarse-textured bread like Pepperidge Farm Original White or Cinnamon Swirl; Bread is dried to better absorb the milk and eggs.

Granny Smith apples are tart and Golden Delicious are mild and sweet. For the best of both worlds, use one of each.

Sautéing the apples enhances flavor and softens their texture.

The cookie recipe can be baked in one large disc, but will be drier and crunchier if baked as single cookies.

The Pecan Praline Cookies are excellent with ice cream!

For a quick and easy caramel sauce, make Brown Sugar Caramel Sauce (page 160).

For a caramelized sugar caramel sauce, make Caramel Sauce (page 178).

Bailey's Chocolate Chip Cheesecake

CAROL'S TIBITS

Chocolate wafers are sold in a long tray and are often on a top shelf in the cookie aisle. If they are unavailable, cream-filled chocolate sandwich cookies may be used; omit the sugar and decrease melted butter to 2 tablespoons.

It will take 35 to 40 wafers to make 1½ cups crumbs. Make the crumbs in a food processor. Add the sugar and butter; process until crumbs begin to clump together.

Bailey's is the best known brand of Irish cream liqueur. It is made of cream, sugar, cocoa powder, and Irish spirits. It is especially tasty with chocolate, caramel, and coffee.

The addition of gelatin to whipped cream stabilizes the cream, preventing weeping if piped onto a dessert too far in advance of serving.

Although appropriate for a St. Patrick's Day celebration, this cheesecake is so delightful you will not want to limit it to a once-a-year occasion. Keep mini cheesecakes on hand in the freezer to soothe your sweet tooth cravings.

Ingredients

Crust
1½ cups chocolate wafer crumbs
¼ cup granulated sugar
6 tablespoons butter, melted

Filling
4 packages (8 ounces each) full-fat cream cheese, at room temp
1½ cups granulated sugar
4 eggs, at room temp
¾ cup Irish cream liqueur
1½ teaspoons vanilla extract
1 cup mini semisweet chocolate chips, divided

Mocha Cream Topping
1 teaspoon unflavored gelatin
2 tablespoons cold water
1 cup (8 ounces) heavy whipping cream
¼ cup powdered sugar
2 tablespoons unsweetened cocoa powder
1½ teaspoons instant espresso powder
Grated chocolate for garnish

Preheat oven to 325°F. Combine wafer crumbs, granulated sugar, and butter; mix until crumbs are moistened and begin to bind together. Press mixture onto bottom of a 10-inch springform pan. Bake 5 to 8 minutes or until crust is puffy; set aside to cool.

Beat cream cheese and sugar in a large mixer bowl on medium speed just until smooth. Add eggs, one at a time, beating on low speed after each addition. Blend in liqueur, vanilla, and ½ cup chips. Pour filling over crust; sprinkle with remaining ½ chips.

Place pan on a sheet of foil to catch any leakage. Bake 1 hour or until center moves only slightly when pan is shaken. Turn oven off and carefully run a knife around the inside of pan to loosen cheesecake and prevent the surface from cracking as it cools. Let cheesecake stand in oven with door ajar for 30 minutes. Cool cheesecake to room temperature before adding topping.

Combine gelatin and water for topping in a small microwave-safe dish; let stand until gelatin absorbs water. Microwave on high just until melted, about 20 seconds; set aside to cool to room temperature. Combine cream, powdered sugar, cocoa, and espresso powder in a mixer bowl; beat until almost thickened. Add dissolved gelatin and beat until thickened. Spread or pipe topping on cheesecake; garnish with grated chocolate. Cover and chill.

Makes 12 to 16 servings

Mini Cheesecake Variation

Prepare crust, filling, and topping for Bailey's Chocolate Chip Cheesecake. Bake as follows: Preheat oven to 325°F. Line 32 muffin cups with foil or paper liners. Press 1 tablespoon crust mixture into each cup. Bake 3 minutes; cool.

Spoon filling into cups, about 2 tablespoons per cup. Sprinkle remaining chocolate chips over filling. Bake 15 to 20 minutes or until filling begins to puff. Cool to room temperature.

Spoon or pipe a generous dollop of topping on each cheesecake. Garnish with grated chocolate. Chill.

Makes 32 mini cheesecakes

Cheesecake Baking Tips

- All ingredients should be room temperature, especially eggs and dairy products. It is best to let them set on the kitchen counter for 20 to 30 minutes before using.

- For easier cutting and transferring baked cheesecakes to serving platters, reverse the bottom of the cheesecake pan. Place the pan on a sheet of foil and wrap the foil around the sides of the pan to catch any leakage during baking.

- Press crumb crusts firmly into the pan with a dry measure cup or back of a spoon. Be careful, however, not to over compact the crumbs or it will be difficult to cut through the crust when served. Crumb crusts will be crispier if baked before adding the filling.

- Use full-fat cream cheese. Reduced-fat cream cheese contains too much moisture for cheesecakes to bake firm enough to slice properly.

- For the desired dense cheesecake texture, do not overbeat cream cheese or eggs. Beat on medium-low or low speed and scrape the bowl sides and beater frequently.

- Break all the eggs into a glass measure or bowl for easy adding to the filling, one at a time.

- Bake cheesecakes until outside edge is dry and slightly puffed but center is still slightly wet in appearance and jiggles when pan is shaken. Cheesecake will continue to bake after the oven is turned off or cake is removed. Slow cooling helps prevent cracks.

- Cheesecakes shrink as they cool. To prevent cracking, run a thin knife or offset spatula around the edge of the cake as soon as it is done baking. Do not remove the springform ring until cake is chilled.

- Cool cheesecakes to room temperature before refrigerating. Lay a paper towel over the top of the pan and then cover with foil to prevent condensation from dripping on the cheesecake.

- Dip serving knife in hot water and wipe dry between cuts.

- Most cheesecakes are high in fat and freeze well for up to two weeks. High moisture cheesecakes may get icy if frozen. Thaw cheesecakes overnight in the refrigerator.

Caramel Toffee Cheesecake

Decadent, Ethereal, Delicious! There are not enough adjectives to describe this cheesecake. It is definitely my favorite and worth the effort to make the caramel sauce. The mini cheesecakes are perfect for a party buffet. Just be sure to make enough for seconds.

Ingredients

Crust

1½ cups graham cracker crumbs (18 squares)

¼ cup firmly packed dark brown sugar

6 tablespoons butter, melted

Filling

4 packages (8 ounces each) full-fat cream cheese, at room temp

1½ cups granulated sugar

5 eggs, at room temperature

2½ teaspoons vanilla extract

2 teaspoons lemon juice

Caramel Sauce and Garnish

1¼ cups granulated sugar

⅓ cup water

2 cups (16 ounces) heavy whipping cream, divided

½ cup (1 stick) butter, cubed

1 teaspoon vanilla extract

2 tablespoons powdered sugar

4 ounces toffee bars, broken into pieces

For crust: Preheat oven to 350°F. Combine crumbs, brown sugar, and butter; stir until crumbs are moistened. Press crumbs onto bottom of a 9-inch springform pan. Bake 5 minutes; set aside to cool.

For filling: Beat cream cheese in a large mixer bowl on medium-low speed just until smooth. Gradually add 1½ cups sugar and beat until smooth. Add eggs, one at a time and beating on low after each addition. Beat in vanilla and lemon juice. Pour filling into crust. Bake 1 to 1¼ hours or until center moves only slightly when shaken. Carefully run a knife around the inside of pan to loosen cheesecake and prevent the surface from cracking as it cools. Cool to room temperature before covering and chilling at least 6 hours.

Continued next page

For the caramel sauce: Heat the 1¼ cups sugar and water in a medium saucepan over low heat, stirring until sugar dissolves. Increase heat and boil without stirring, but frequently brushing down sides of pan with a wet pastry brush and swirling pan occasionally until sauce turns a deep amber color, about 8 minutes. Reduce heat to very low. Add 1 cup of the heavy cream (mixture will bubble vigorously and caramel will harden). Stir until caramel is smooth. Gradually whisk in butter. Cool slightly; add vanilla.

Remove chilled cheesecake from pan and place on serving plate. Spoon enough caramel sauce in center to cover top of cheesecake. Cover remaining sauce and chill until serving time. Chill cheesecake until topping is set, about 2 hours.

For garnish: Whip remaining 1 cup heavy cream and powdered sugar until stiff. Pipe whipped cream around edge of cheesecake and garnish with toffee pieces. Serve with remaining caramel sauce, warmed in microwave until butter is melted in the sauce.

Makes 12 to 16 servings

Mini Caramel Toffee Cheesecakes

Prepare crust, filling, and topping for Caramel Toffee Cheesecake; bake as follows:

Preheat oven to 325°F. Line 32 muffin cups with foil or paper liners. Press 1 tablespoon crust mixture into each cup. Bake 3 minutes; cool.

Spoon filling into cups, about 2 tablespoons per cup. Bake 15 to 20 minutes; cool to room temperature.

Spread about a teaspoon of cooled caramel topping on each cake; chill until topping is set. Top with a dollop of whipped cream and crushed toffee.

Makes 32 mini cheesecakes

Chocolate Chip Cookies

CAROL'S TIDBITS

If you need cookies in a hurry, spread the dough in a 10x15x1-inch baking sheet. Bake 15 to 18 minutes until golden brown. Cut into squares while still warm.

Most everyone has a favorite chocolate chip cookie recipe. Our family likes cookies with crispy edges and chewy centers. This is our favorite recipe. It probably isn't much different from everyone else's, but subtle differences sometimes make big differences in baked cookies.

Ingredients

½ cup (1 stick) butter, at room temp
½ cup butter-flavored solid vegetable shortening
1 cup granulated sugar
½ cup firmly packed brown sugar
2 eggs, at room temp

2 teaspoons vanilla extract
2 cups plus 2 tablespoons flour
1 teaspoon baking soda
1 teaspoon salt
1 package (12 ounces) semisweet chocolate chips

Combine butter, shortening, and sugars in a mixer bowl; beat on medium-high speed until light and fluffy. Beat in eggs and vanilla. Combine flour, baking soda, and salt; add to creamed mixture and beat on low speed. Stir in chocolate chips. Cover dough and chill several hours.

Preheat oven to 375°F. Drop dough from teaspoons or small ice cream/cookie scoop onto parchment-lined baking sheets. Bake for 10 to 12 minutes or until cookies are golden brown around the edges. Remove cookies from oven; let stand 2 minutes before transferring to a wire rack.

Makes about 4 dozen cookies

Warm Salted Caramel Cookie Sundaes

For an absolutely scrumptious dessert, make extra large cookies using ¼ cup cookie dough. Bake 12 to 15 minutes until golden brown on the edges and slightly soft in the center. Transfer cookies to individual serving plates, top with a large scoop of ice cream, drizzle with caramel sauce and sprinkle with coarse salt. Yummy!

Cookie Baking Tips

- Cookies made with butter will spread more and be thinner. Cookies made with solid vegetable shortening will spread less and be thicker.

- I use half butter and half shortening to get a baked cookie with a spread in between butter and shortening; cookies made with margarine (must have a fat content of 80%) will bake similarly. Cookies made with vegetable spreads are unpredictable.

- All-butter cookies have the best flavor. The use of butter-flavored shortening versus unflavored shortening is personal preference.

- Butter and shortening should be set out at room temperature for 20 to 30 minutes before creaming to hold air properly for the best texture.

- Granulated sugar makes cookies hard and crisp. Brown sugar makes cookies soften upon standing.

- Use pasteurized eggs for food safety anytime uncooked dough will be eaten. It is often difficult to resist eating the dough; I know of a time, or two, when more of the dough was eaten than was baked.

- Chilling the dough at least one hour before baking controls spreading and makes cookies have a better texture.

- Cookies bake the best on aluminum baking sheets without sides. Lining the sheets with parchment controls spreading and sticking, and makes clean up very easy.

- I like to push a small off-set spatula against the edge of cookies as soon as removed from the oven to make them more rounded and to get a crinkly appearance in the center.

Gingerbread Cookies

CAROL'S TIDBITS

Be sure to use pasteurized eggs if you snack on raw cookie dough.

Nearly every country in Europe has its own name for centuries-old gingerbread traditions.

Ginger aids digestion and a gingerbread cookie after a large holiday meal is the secret to a good night's sleep.

Hosts at a resort near Branson, Missouri leave ginger cookies on their guests' pillows every night.

The beauty of this dough is that the scraps from cutting out cookies can be chilled and rerolled several times.

Add additional flour to dough if using it to make gingerbread houses.

Bake a tradition with this recipe for crisp, spicy gingerbread cookies. It is a great dough for making gingerbread people and houses; it is so easy to work with and leaves a wonderful aroma throughout the house as it bakes. I tied them to ribbons to make Advent calendars for our sons. They have long outgrown the calendars, but I still make these cookies every Christmas.

Ingredients

¾ cup sugar
½ cup solid vegetable shortening
1 egg
¼ cup molasses
1½ teaspoons baking soda
¼ cup water
3 cups flour

¾ teaspoon ground cinnamon
½ teaspoon salt
½ teaspoon ground ginger
½ teaspoon ground cloves
Additional flour as needed,
    about ¼ cup

Combine sugar, shortening, egg, and molasses in a large mixer bowl; beat on medium-high speed until light and creamy. Dissolve baking soda in water; stir into creamed mixture (mixture will look curdled). Combine the 3 cups flour with cinnamon, ginger, cloves, and salt on wax paper; add to creamed mixture on low speed. Cover and chill overnight.

Preheat oven to 375°F. Turn dough out onto floured surface and knead in additional flour as needed until dough is no longer sticky. Roll dough about ⅛-inch thick and cut out gingerbread cookies with floured cutters. Place about 1 inch apart on a parchment-lined baking sheet. Bake 8 to 10 minutes or until lightly browned and firm to the touch. Transfer cookies to a wire rack to cool.

Makes about 100 miniature or 3 dozen large gingerbread boys or girls

Holiday Peppernuts

I know Christmas is near when I am asked, "When are you going to make the peppernuts?" We love the spicy-sweet flavor and crunchy texture of these cookie nuggets flavored with cardamom and anise, not pepper as the name suggests. They are reminiscent of the walnut-size pfeffernüsse Grandma made every year and were dunked in coffee to soften. These are the size of marbles, can be eaten as a snack, and no coffee is required!

Ingredients

¾ cup granulated sugar
⅔ cup dark corn syrup
¼ cup milk
¼ cup solid vegetable shortening
½ teaspoon baking powder
½ to ¾ teaspoon ground cardamom
¼ teaspoon salt

¼ teaspoon ground cloves
½ teaspoon anise oil or 1 teaspoon anise extract
½ teaspoon vanilla extract
3¾ cups flour
Powdered sugar

Combine sugar, corn syrup, milk and shortening in a large saucepan; bring to a boil over medium-high heat. Remove from heat and cool for 10 minutes.

Stir in baking powder, cardamom, salt, cloves, anise oil and vanilla. Add flour about a cup at a time, kneading in the last addition on a floured surface to make stiff dough. The dough ball should be very smooth and almost slip as it is being kneaded.

Lightly sprinkle work surface with powdered sugar. Divide dough into small portions, about ¼ to ½ cup each. Roll each portion with the palms of your hands to form ropes about ⅜ inch thick. Place ropes on a tray, cover with foil, and chill until firm.

Preheat oven to 375°F. Cut each rope into pieces about ⅜ inch long. Bake on parchment-lined baking sheets for 12 to 15 minutes or until lightly browned. Cool 1 to 2 minutes before removing from baking sheet into a tray.

Makes 6 cups

CAROL'S TIDBITS

Pfeffernüsse translates as both gingernuts and peppernuts.

Pepper was the hottest and most expensive spice in the Middle Ages and it became a collective term for all exotic spices which were imported from distant lands.

Cardamom, a member of the ginger family, has a spicy-sweet flavor and is frequently used in northern European and East Indian cooking.

Anise has a sweet licorice flavor. Anise oil can be found in craft stores where cake decorating supplies are sold and at some pharmacies. It is preferred to anise extract because its flavor is more concentrated.

Acknowledgements

Some of the recipes in this book were inspired by or adapted from country inn or restaurant recipes for use in my Country Inn Christmas classes. My thanks goes to the following establishments:

Abbington Manor; Latte, SC: Baby Greens with Goat Cheese Medallions

Belle Grae Inn; Staunton, VA: Roast Pork Loin with Orange Honey Glaze

Buffalo Mountain Lodge; Banff, Alberta: Celery Root Mashed Potatoes

Calmar Guest House; Calmar, IA: Cranberry Wine Salad

Captain Daniel Packer Inne; Mystic, CN: Bailey's Chocolate Chip Cheesecake

Castle Marne; Denver, CO: Rum Cake with Crème Anglaise

Delta Queen; New Orleans, LA: Minnesota Wild Rice Soup

DesBarres Manor House; Guysborough, Nova Scotia: Smashed Red Potatoes with Parmesan Basil Butter

Glen Ellen Inn Restaurant; Sonoma, CA: Cinnamon-Bread Pudding

Harbor House Bed & Breakfast; Georgetown, SC: Southern Shrimp and Grits

Harbor House Inn by the Sea; Elk, CA: Gingered Apple Crisp

Herren House; Waynesville, NC: Blackberry-Glazed Pork Tenderloin

Highland Lake Inn; Flat Rock, NC: Curried Butternut Squash with Apples and Sausage

Jared Coffin House; Nantucket Island, MA: Spicy Cranberry Muffins

LaGrange Plantation Inn; Henderson, NC: Spanakopita Bites

Lake Yellowstone Hotel; Yellowstone National Park, WY: Crostini with White Bean Hummus, Baked Mushrooms, and Roasted Peppers

Magnolias; Charleston, SC: Brown Sugar Caramel Sauce

Marco's Supperclub; Seattle, WA: Greens with Roasted Beets and Goat Cheese

Nemacolin Woodlands Resort; Farmington, PA: Roast Turkey Tenderloin with Sweet Potato and Apple Hash

Old Drover's Inn: Dover Plains, NY: Bourbon Sauce

Olde Port Inn; Port San Luis, CA: Caramel Toffee Cheesecake

Philbrook Farm Inn; Shelburne, NH: New England Brown Bread

Rabbit Hill Inn; Lower Waterford, VT: Grand Marnier Chocolate Cobbler; Warm Apple Bread Pudding with Pecan Praline Crust

Ravenscroft Inn; Port Townsend, WA: Double-Mushroom Bread Pudding

Rowe Inn; Ellsworth MA: White Chocolate Brownies

Rowell's 1820 Inn; Simonsville, VT: Mixed Greens with Maple Bacon Dressing

Sharrow Bay Country House; Lake District, England: Sticky Toffee Pudding

Steamboat Inn; Steamboat, OR: Brussel Sprouts with Carrots and Rosemary; Gingerbread Cake with Caramelized Pears; Walnut Rice

The Beach House Restaurant; Marbella, Spain: Manchego Cheese, Tomato and Basil Tart

The Captain Whidbey Inn; Coupeville, WA: Whidbey Island Smoked Salmon Mousse

The Fearrington House; Chapel Hill, NC: Green Beans with Toasted Garlic Bread Crumbs; Sauteen Summer Squash with Tomatoes and Basil

The Hubbell House; Mantorville, MN: Heartland Crab Cakes

The Inn at Fordhook Farm; Doylestown, PA: Cranberry Scones

The Inn at Kristofer's; Sister Bay, WI: Door County Salad with Maple Balsamic Vinaigrette; Maple Butternut Squash Bisque

The Inn at Phillips Mill; New Hope, PA: Puréed Sweet Potatoes

The Mainstay Inn; Cape May; NJ: Almond Coffee Cake

The Marquesa Hotel; Key West, FL: Blueberry-Banana Bread

The Scottish Lion Inn; North Conway, NH: Rumbledethumps

The Shire Inn; Chelsea, VT: Baked Amaretti-Stuffed Pears

The White Inn; Fredonia, NY: Irish Beef Tenders

The Wildwood Inn; Ware, MA: Honey Raisin Brown Bread

Three Village Inn; Stoney Brook, NY: Cold Cauliflower Nivernais

Timberline Lodge; Mt. Hood, OR: Pan-Seared Breast of Chicken with Wild Mushrooms & Sherry Sauce

Wickwood Inn; Saugatuck, MI: Carrot Cake with Cream Cheese Crème

Recipe Index